CONTAINER GARDENING

DAVID SQUIRE

CONTAINER GARDENING

DAVID SQUIRE

Illustrated by Vana Haggerty

TIGER BOOKS INTERNATIONAL
LONDON

Designed and conceived by

THE BRIDGEWATER BOOK COMPANY LTD

Art Directed by PETER BRIDGEWATER

Designed by TERRY JEAVONS

Illustrated by VANA HAGGERTY FLS

Edited by MARGOT RICHARDSON

CLB 3376

This edition published in 1994 by

TIGER BOOKS INTERNATIONAL PLC, London

Printed and bound in Singapore

ISBN 1-85501-386-X

CONTENTS

FROM ANCIENT TO MODERN

FROM early times, particularly in China, people have grown plants in pots. Indeed, bonsai, the method of growing artificially dwarfed plants in small containers, was begun by the Chinese and later turned into an art by the Japanese. This craft is thought to have originated more than one thousand years ago.

Early earthenware pots were probably made from strips of clay, moulded and fused together. Later, the potter's wheel was invented by the Egyptians, and pots of all kinds could then be produced more quickly and easily. Early flowerpots were small and used in clusters, either surrounding buildings or hanging from walls in a style much suited to hot, Mediterranean countries. Later, during the Italian Renaissance, larger and more ornate types were used, developing into features of decorative and architectural value, as much as for growing plants.

As the desire to grow tender plants spread northwards throughout Europe, the pot evolved into a tub. It was the French garden designer André Le Nôtre who, in the mid-seventeenth century at Versailles, showed an unrivalled fervour for tubs, mainly as a way to grow orange trees which each spring had to be moved from their covered winter quarters to positions outdoors. The large, square, lead or slate containers became known as Versailles planters. Each tub weighed a tonne/ton or more and required special, low trolleys to move them.

Orange trees were introduced from France to Britain in 1562 and initially heated 'sheds' were erected over them in winter.

DURING *the eighteenth century, orange trees were wheeled out of doors on low, small-wheel trucks at the beginning of summer to join permanent planting schemes. In autumn, they would be returned indoors. The task was labour intensive.*

Later, they too were planted in containers. In the eighteenth century, wooden containers were designed with removable sides so that soil and roots could be inspected for health.

THE *tradition of growing trees in large tubs continues. Here they are seen in rigid lines in the Cloister Court of Lincoln Cathedral. Many religious places had long traditions of growing plants.*

ROUND TUBS

Large, round tubs, so often seen today, are more recent than square types, but they must have been popular in the early eighteenth century as the frontispiece to Thomas Fairchild's 1722 book, *The City Gardener*, reveals many plants in them, including the Mexican *Agave americana*. A catalogue, issued by The Society of Gardeners in 1739, illustrates plants in urns, while early North American gardening books reveal a passion for putting plants in pots. Their use was strongly influenced by the immigrants from Mediterranean countries, who had long grown plants in containers.

A more recent development has been the use of large, low, shallow, vandal-proof concrete containers for growing plants in streets in summer, an idea originated by the parks department in Stockholm. This theme has spread to many towns and cities throughout the world.

EARLY NURSERY PLANTS

During the eighteenth century, many nurseries flourished in London, but in the early part of the following century their existence within an increasingly metropolitan landscape became threatened. One of the most important nurseries was The Loddiges, which closed in 1852 with a general sale of stock. Many trees and shrubs were bought by The Crystal Palace Company, for planting in the Crystal Palace Park. Here is the removal of a large palm tree.

RANGE OF POTS, TUBS AND URNS

PLANTS can be grown in almost any container, as long as it is strong enough to support the weight of compost and plants. However, it must also have a pleasing appearance, harmonizing with the plants and blending with its surroundings. Apart from aesthetic considerations, outdoor containers must be able to withstand frost, rain, snow and hot sunshine, to say nothing of the boisterous activities of children and large, excitable dogs.

In addition to traditional containers, growing-bags create colour when planted with a range of spring-flowering bulbs or summer-blooming plants. Patterned bags create brighter backgrounds than plain ones, but even so they are not as attractive as pots and tubs. However, trailing plants soon camouflage their edges.

Stone sinks offer the chance to grow small rock-garden plants, even on town patios where space is scarce. They also make homes for dwarf, slow-growing conifers, miniature spring bulbs and small, evergreen shrubs.

Vegetables need not be neglected on patios; specialist containers for strawberry plants are available, as well as traditional strawberry pots with planting holes in their

MOVEABLE SIDES

During the early eighteenth century, Charles McIntosh designed an orange tub that could be taken apart to allow roots of trees and shrubs to be inspected. It also made the task of repotting a great deal easier.

RECTANGULAR, *metal or stone containers form strong bases for climbers such as large-flowered clematis. Metal becomes hot in summer, so be prepared to water frequently.*

ORNATE *and figured terracotta pots look superb. Use lax, trailing plants such as nasturtiums to soften their rims and sides, but take care not to completely cloak them and hide attractive features.*

SQUARE, *wooden tubs have a dignity not conferred on round tubs, probably because early containers at Versailles had a similar shape. Here, one is planted with an agapanthus.*

ROUND, *wooden tubs form strong bases for shrubs and small trees; they are also superb for massed plantings of spring-flowering bulbs. Plant a colourful medley of different species.*

A BULB *or multiple planter – now frequently available in heavy-duty plastic – is ideal for growing small bulbs. These pots are also made in terracotta and reconstituted stone.*

CONCRETE *containers need not be heavy and dominant. Here is a small bowl set on a pedestal. Take special care not to drop one as it will smash. They become hot in summer.*

sides and tops. Alternatively, cut holes in a pensioned-off beer barrel (see page 48).

Proprietary tubs for growing potatoes are available, with the advantage of being collapsible for storage in winter. Large plastic pots – or buckets with holes pierced in their bases – are ideal as containers for tomato plants. Runner beans are candidates for growing-bags, but ensure a supporting wire framework is available, as canes cannot normally be pushed into the bags.

Garden centres and high street shops offer a wide range of containers, especially in spring and early summer. If they are carefully used and stored in winter, when not in use, they last for many seasons. Thin plastic containers, however, are much more vulnerable to deterioration than thicker ones which, although more expensive, may prove to be a better buy.

CAR *tyres can be given a new lease of life by securing them in a stack and growing plants in a bucket placed in its top. Paint the tyres matt white to create a contrast with the plants.*

OLD *or broken wheelbarrows create eye-catching features when planted with a mixture of summer-flowering plants. Wooden barrows have a softer outline than metal types.*

LARGE, *wooden boxes are ideal for perennial plants, such as hostas. These containers, with their soft outlines, harmonize well with large-leaved and informal plants.*

MATERIALS FOR CONTAINERS

THE RANGE of materials used to make garden containers is wide and extends from traditional types, such as wood and stone, to more recent ones like plastic and fibreglass. Each material has merits and disadvantages, as well as the types of plants and surrounds that are most suitable for it.

- Plastic has a clean, clinical appearance that especially suits formal, modern gardens. Containers include pots and planters of all sizes, as well as corner (quadrant) containers and square, Versailles-like tubs. Some are white and bright, while others are in grey, brown or black. Their durability depends on the thickness of the plastic.
- Fibreglass has many excellent qualities and can be formed into a wide range of designs and patterns. It does not decay, but is unable to withstand sharp knocks. Like plastic, fibreglass warms up rapidly, and special care is needed to ensure composts remain cool and well-watered during the heat of summer.

COADE STONE

In 1769, George and Eleanor Coade bought a factory which made terracotta-type artificial stone. Soon after, George died but Eleanor and her daughter experimented, added further ingredients and originated a weatherproof material, less easily eroded than natural stone.

They produced superbly designed figures and decorations which became much desired. The daughter died in 1821 and the factory closed in 1840. Unfortunately, the formula for the mixture was lost. The stone was also used on buildings.

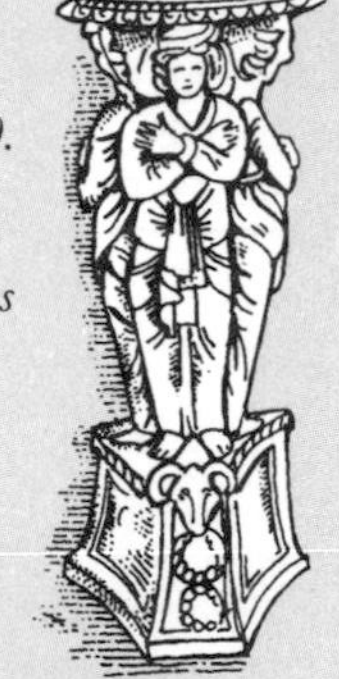

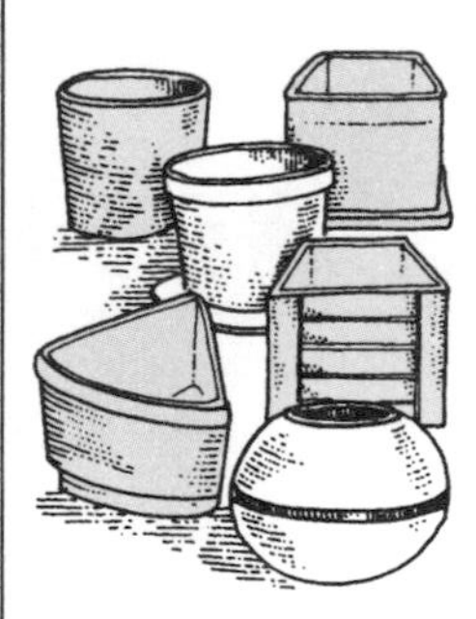

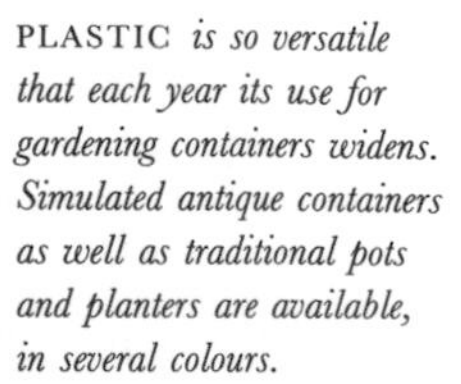

PLASTIC *is so versatile that each year its use for gardening containers widens. Simulated antique containers as well as traditional pots and planters are available, in several colours.*

WOODEN *containers have a soft, natural appearance. Most of them are formed from softwood and protected with plant-friendly wood preservatives. More expensive ones are made of hardwood.*

TRADITIONAL *jardinières were made of lead; today they are replicated in fibreglass. Aluminium is sometimes used for containers, but metal is hot in summer and cold in winter.*

CONCRETE *containers have a clinical, modern appearance and do not harmonize in informal, rustic settings. Because their sides are usually thick, the containers are almost always quite heavy.*

RECONSTITUTED *stone containers range from jardinières to urns, vases and troughs. Highly ornate surfaces and shapes are possible. They are very durable and soon assume a weathered appearance.*

EARTHENWARE *containers range widely in size and shape, the colour harmonizing with most plants. They are especially attractive in informal settings, and look good when in groups.*

- Wooden tubs and planters are superb for plants that remain outside all year: compost in them remains slightly insulated from temperature extremes. Shrubs, small trees and herbaceous perennials are especially suited to tubs.
- Clay pots have traditionally been used for plants; they are porous, decorative and offer insulation from extreme heat. Water evaporating through the pots keeps the compost and roots cool. If dropped they usually break, and are best placed under cover in winter when not in use.
- Natural stone containers are unsurpassable, but expensive and scarce. Shallow, old stone sinks are superb – if you acquire one, treasure it for life.
- Reconstituted stone is increasingly popular and used to create variously shaped containers. It is also used to form attractive statues. They are durable, and after a few years the surface colour mellows. Clean them with water and a soft brush. Do not use wire brushes, as they will damage the surface badly and could, eventually, remove decorative patterns.

FIBREGLASS *containers are varied and often given intricate patterns, sometimes to replicate wood or lead. They are light to handle, but must not be dropped, or they will break.*

SHALLOW, *old stone sinks create superb miniature gardens for alpines, miniature conifers and small evergreen shrubs. Glazed sinks can be given a rustic, weathered appearance* *(see page 50)*.

BRONZE *urns are sometimes available, often replicas of containers made during the mid-Georgian period. They are expensive, incomparable and desirable. Use them as special features in a garden.*

POSITIONING CONTAINERS

SELECT containers to suit your garden, rather than finding an attractive pot, tub or urn and then being unable to position it in a sympathetic setting. For example, clinically-outlined, dish-like concrete containers are ideal for placing on bright, formal patios, but not in informal woodland settings. Wooden tubs are better for rustic, rural positions.

TRICKY STATUES!

Trick fountains were popular in Renaissance gardens, with balls appearing to be raised on spouts of water. Other inventive garden features were statues of naked people that were connected to a tap so that water could suddenly squirt at innocent passers-by.

PERSPECTIVE AND MASS

Containers on patios are invariably admired from nearby positions, but those in gardens sometimes create focal points. Others are merged in groups. Those that create focal points need positioning with care to ensure they fulfil this role, rather than obscuring other features. For example, if there is a tall hedge at the bottom of a garden, an urn festooned with summer flowers and placed on a tall pedestal in front of it will soon attract the eye. It will also create attention and be attractive if positioned two-thirds of the way down a garden, with an uncluttered background. However, it will not be attractive and a focal point if tall and placed only a small way down a garden. Small, low containers are better in this position.

SMALL *courtyards are enhanced by evergreen shrubs in tubs or other large containers. Such sheltered places enable slightly tender plants to be grown.*

GROUPINGS *of pots and tubs at the tops of steps help to create focal points and to direct people to entrances. Small containers always look best when in groups.*

USE *combinations of large, dominant pots and troughs to hide unattractive features, such as drainage pipes. Alternatively, position them to act as focal points.*

SEASONAL OR PERMANENT?

Where a dominant feature is needed throughout the year, shrubs with evergreen foliage are essential, especially those with variegated leaves. Plant them in large, wooden tubs to help protect their roots from excessively cold weather. Bay trees *(Laurus nobilis)* are evergreen, and especially eye-catching when grown with clear stems up to about 1.2m/4ft high, planted in white tubs and positioned either side of an entrance. Small, evergreen, variegated shrubs, such as *Hebe franciscana* 'Variegata', are also good for providing colour in winter.

Containers such as shallow urns and those made of thin plastic are best when planted in late spring with summer-flowering bedding plants. Once the display is over, plants and compost are removed and the container cleaned and stored until the following year. If permanent plants are planted in them, their roots will soon be damaged by cold weather. Herbaceous perennials, such as hostas and agapanthus, are soon killed when planted with little soil.

Spring-flowering bulbs, which are planted in early autumn, also suffer if the soil is too shallow and subsequently freezes. They are best planted in tubs and positioned near to a house, where they can be easily admired in spring, whatever the weather.

DECORATIVE URNS

A few urns are not designed to be filled with plants, but nevertheless are ideal for creating interest alongside drives or perhaps in long, hedge-like beds of low-growing lavender. They are usually made of reconstituted stone and after mellowing harmonize with the spiky, deep-purple flowers of Lavandula *'Hidcote'. Bronze urns are available, but are too dominant and seldom form pleasing partnerships with plants immediately around them. In any case, stone has a more natural appearance.*

A GARDEN *bench with containers formed of car tyres positioned either side helps to reduce the blandness of long hedges. The displays can be changed at the beginning of spring and summer.*

ENTRANCES *benefit from a few shrubs in large pots or tubs, highlighted by seasonal flowering plants. Small-leaved, variegated ivies enrich the scene with colour throughout the year.*

STONE *urns on pedestals create height and focal points in lawns and long, wide paths. Fill the bowl-shaped container with spreading and trailing foliage and summer-flowering plants.*

SPRING-FLOWERING PLANTS

SPRING displays are important in gardens; in a trice they remove winter gloom and introduce many bright, varied colours. However, unlike summer-flowering bedding plants that produce a glowing display almost from the moment they are planted, spring-flowering types are invariably biennial. This means they are raised from seed sown during the previous summer and are planted into containers in late summer or early autumn.

Bulbs are other candidates for spring colour, and those such as daffodils and tulips are planted at the same time as biennial plants.

> DAY'S-EYE
>
> *Widely known to the sixteenth-century English herbalist John Gerard as Bruisewort, the Daisy was earlier called Daezeseze and later Day's-eye. Romantically, it is sometimes referred to as Measure of Love, because lovers pulled off its petals to the count of 'he loves me, he loves me not'. However, the daisy gains its botanical name, Bellis, from the Latin word for war, because an ointment made from it was used to staunch wounds on battlefields.*

GUIDELINES FOR SPRING COLOUR

Spring displays must be bold to create strong colour impact. Here are a few ways to achieve this:

- When planting daffodils in tubs, create dominant displays by planting bulbs in two layers, with the bases of the upper bulbs nestling in the gaps between the noses of the lower ones. This method also creates a mass of stems which are better able to resist strong winds in exposed places.
- When planting bulbs, it is better to pack one container with them than to spread out the same number in several tubs. Remember that bulbs do not spread out in the same way as bedding plants.
- Never plant bulbs that look damaged or diseased; they will not flower and subsequently leave gaps in the display.

POLYANTHUSES (Primula polyantha) *are superb on their own or when mixed with spring-flowering bulbs. Buy plants in early autumn or sow outdoors in seed-beds in late spring.*

WALLFLOWERS (Cheiranthus cheiri *and* Erysimum *x* allionii) *are suitable for tubs or large bowls. Buy plants in autumn or sow seeds outdoors in late spring or early summer.*

PANSIES (Viola *x* wittrockiana)*; several types, flowering through winter to spring, others in summer. Buy plants in autumn or sow seeds outdoors in early summer.*

• If you live in an exposed area, use plenty of compact bedding plants, such as daisies and pansies; they are less likely to be damaged by strong winds. They also help to create colour around the bases of tulips and daffodils.

• Large containers planted with bulbs and spring-flowering bedding plants sometimes look rather uninteresting in late autumn and winter. Therefore, use small evergreen shrubs or perhaps some variegated small-leaved ivies to provide colour throughout winter.

• Group plants that, when combined, have a long flowering period. For example, Forget-me-nots carry on an attractive display after early-flowering tulips have finished creating their display.

• Spring-flowering displays are often short-lived. Therefore, grow a few pots of other bulbs or primroses which can be transferred to the main display if bare spaces unexpectedly occur.

• In large tubs with summer-flowering shrubs, use coloured-leaved, ground-covering plants, such as *Lamium maculatum* 'Aureum' with golden leaves, to create extra colour during spring as well as throughout summer.

NAPOLEON AND VIOLETS

Napoleon was an admirer of violets and gave bouquets of them to Josephine on their wedding anniversaries. When banished to Elba he said "I will return with the violets in the spring". Immediately, violets became the symbol of the Bonapartists and he became known and 'Père Violet'. Before he was exiled to St. Helena after his defeat at Waterloo in 1811, he is said to have visited Josephine's grave and picked their favourite flower. After he died, a locket he was wearing was found to contain a small lock of her hair and a few ancient, dried violets.

FORGET-ME-NOTS (Myosotis alpestris) *are ideal on their own or with short tulips. Buy plants in autumn or sow seeds outdoors during early summer. Use a large tub.*

DAFFODILS *(large-trumpeted narcissi) are the epitome of spring and look superb in tubs or troughs, on their own or with polyanthus. Plant new bulbs in late summer or early autumn.*

DAISIES (Bellis perennis) *in their double-flowered form create superb backcloths for daffodils and tulips in tubs and large bowls. Buy plants in autumn, or sow outdoors in early summer.*

ANNUALS FOR POTS AND TUBS 1

ANNUALS are plants that are raised from seeds each year, and then planted either into borders or containers on patios. When considering varieties for growing in containers, always select those with short, bushy natures. And make sure they are well developed and will soon (if not immediately) break into flower after planting.

RAISING PLANTS

• Floss Flower *(Ageratum houstonianum):* Sow seeds 3mm/1/8in deep in early spring in 10–16°C/50–61°F. Germination takes ten to fourteen days. When large enough to handle, prick off into seed-trays and later acclimatize plants to outdoor conditions. Plant outside when all risk of frost has passed.

• Sweet Alyssum *(Alyssum maritimum/Lobularia maritima:* Sow seeds 6mm/1/4in deep during late winter and early spring in 10–13°C/50–55°F. Germination takes seven to ten days. Prick out the seedlings in small clusters, slowly acclimatize to outdoor temperatures and plant into a container.

• Love-lies-bleeding *(Amaranthus caudatus):* Can be sown directly into hardy annual borders, but for planting into containers sow seed 3mm/1/8in deep in late winter or early spring in 10–13°C/50–55°F. Germination takes two to three weeks. Prick out seedlings into

POT MARIGOLD

This Southern European, bushy annual has long been grown for its medicinal value: a conserve made from it was known to be a 'cureth in the trembling of the harts'. The flowers were also used to give cheese a yellow colour, while it was said that if you looked 'wyscely' on the marigold early in the morning it would preserve you from 'feveres' during the day.

AGERATUM houstonianum: *Height 13–30cm/5–12in, plant 13–20cm/5–8in apart. Clustered heads of blue, pink or white, flowers like powder-puffs, from early to late summer.*

ALYSSUM maritimum (*now* Lobularia maritima)*: Height 7.5–15cm/3–6in, plant 15–20cm/6–8in apart. Carpeting and trailing, in white, rosy-red and deep purple throughout summer.*

AMARANTHUS caudatus *(Love-lies-bleeding): Height 38–60cm/15–24in, plant 30–45cm/12–18in apart. Trailing red, maroon or green tassels, mid to late summer. Large tubs only.*

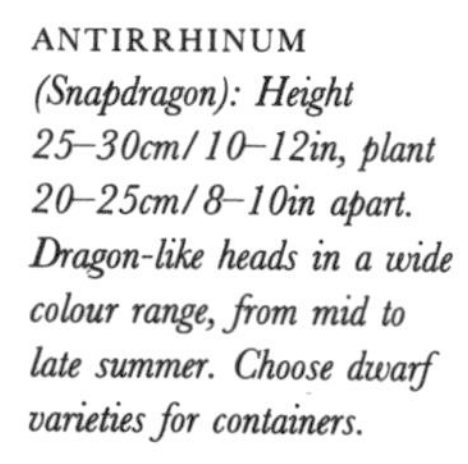

ANTIRRHINUM *(Snapdragon): Height 25–30cm/10–12in, plant 20–25cm/8–10in apart. Dragon-like heads in a wide colour range, from mid to late summer. Choose dwarf varieties for containers.*

BEGONIA semperflorens *(Wax Flower): Height 15–23cm/6–9in, plant 15–20cm/6–8in apart. Low, bushy plants, smothered in scarlet, pink or white flowers from early to late summer.*

CALENDULA officinalis *(Pot Marigold): Height 30–45cm/12–18in, plant 23–38cm/9–15in apart. Wide colour range, mainly yellow and orange, from early to late summer. Use dwarf types.*

small pots and slowly acclimatize them to outdoor conditions.

- Snapdragon *(Antirrhinum majus)*: Sow seeds 3mm/1/8in deep during late winter or early spring in 16–20°C/61–68°C. Prick off seedlings into seed-trays and later acclimatize to outdoor conditions.
- Wax Flower *(Begonia semperflorens)*: Sow seeds thinly on the surface of compost (do not cover) during late winter and early spring. Water lightly with a fine-rosed can and place in 16–20°C/61–68°F. Germination takes two to four weeks. Prick off the seedlings into small clusters and slowly acclimatize them to outdoor conditions.
- Pot Marigold *(Calendula officinalis)*: Mostly, it is sown directly into hardy-annual borders, but sow seeds in pots 6mm/1/4in deep in 15°C/59°F during early to mid-spring. Transfer the seedlings to small pots and acclimatize to outdoor conditions.

Alternatively, sow two or three seeds in a small pot, later thinning to the strongest seedling.

MIXING AND MATCHING

Creating medleys of plants with flower colours that blend is increasingly popular. Here are a few of them to try:

- *An edging of white, trailing alyssum with a bright colour range of antirrhinums positioned in the centre.*
- *Plant rose-red trailing alyssum around the sides of containers, with Pot Marigolds in the centre. Both of these flowers create colour over a long period.*
- *Plant pink-flowering varieties of* Begonia semperflorens *in the centre of an urn, with blue, trailing lobelia around the edges.*
- *White-flowered forms of* Begonia semperflorens *with copper-colour foliage harmonize with the rich colour of earthenware pots. There are also pink, scarlet and red-flowered types, which can be used to create contrasts with other flowers in containers.*

ANNUALS FOR POTS AND TUBS 2

THE RANGE of annuals that flower beautifully in containers is extensive and includes some more unusual plants.

Many seed companies specialize in plants suitable for growing in containers and devote parts of their catalogues specifically to them. Each year, new varieties are introduced, many especially suited for planting in containers.

RAISING PLANTS

- Feverfew *(Chrysanthemum parthenium/Matricaria eximia)*: Sow seeds 3mm/1/8in deep in late winter and early spring in 16–20°C/61–68°F. Germination takes ten to fourteen days. When large enough to handle, prick off the seedlings into seed-trays and slowly acclimatize them to outdoor conditions. Plant into containers when all risk of frost has passed. They are ideal for planting in containers in areas exposed to wind.
- Dusty Miller *(Cineraria maritima/Senecio bicolor)*: Sow seeds 3mm/1/8in deep from late winter to mid-spring in 16–20°F/61–68°F. Germination takes ten to fourteen days. When large enough to handle, transfer the seedlings to seed-trays and slowly harden off.
- Tickseed *(Coreopsis tinctoria)*: Sow seeds 3mm/1/8in deep in early spring in 16°C/61°F. Germination normally takes ten to fourteen days. When large enough to handle, move the seedlings into small pots and slowly acclimatize them to outdoor conditions.

COREOPSIS

These are all North American plants; some are herbaceous perennials, but Coreopsis tinctoria *is an annual. They are collectively known as tickseeds, with* Coreopsis leavenworthii *once being used by North American Indians to treat heat exhaustion.*

CHRYSANTHEMUM parthenium *(Feverfew): Height 23–45cm/9–18in, plant 15–25cm/6–10in apart. Bushy plants with small, rounded flower heads, in white or golden-yellow, from early to late summer.*

CINERARIA maritima/Senecio bicolor *(Dusty Miller): Height 45–60cm/1½–2ft, plant 30–38cm/12–15in apart. Leaves covered with white, woolly hairs. Several varieties, some with deeply cut leaves.*

COREOPSIS tinctoria *(Calliopsis): Dwarf varieties only. Height 30–38cm/12–15in, plant 20–25cm/8–10in apart. Bushy, with stiff stems bearing yellow to chestnut flowers from mid to late summer.*

• Kingfisher Daisy *(Felicia bergeriana)*: Sow seeds 3mm/1/8in deep from late winter to mid-spring in 10–15°C/50–59°F. Germination takes two to three weeks – sometimes longer. When large enough to handle, prick off the seedlings into seed-trays and later acclimatize to outdoor conditions.

• Busy Lizzie *(Impatiens)*: Sow seeds 3mm/1/8in deep during early and mid-spring in 15–20°C/59–68°F. Germination takes two to three weeks. When large enough to handle, prick out the seedlings into seed-trays, acclimatize to outdoor conditions and plant into suitable pots after all risk of frost has passed.

• Burning Bush/Summer Cypress (*Kochia scoparia* 'Trichophylla'): Sow seeds 3mm/1/8in deep during early and mid-spring in 15–20°C/59–68°F. Germination is rapid, taking only five to seven days. When large enough to handle, transfer the seedlings into seed-trays, and then plant into larger containers only after all risk of frost has passed.

MIXING AND MATCHING

• *In large tubs, use* Cineraria maritima (Senecio bicolor) *as a centre plant with* Chrysanthemum parthenium *'Golden Ball' around the edges.*

• *Use* Chrysanthemum parthenium *as an edging to red pelargoniums.*

• Felicia bergeriana *looks good in a medley of other annuals in large tubs. Their bright faces are best when seen from above.*

• *Busy Lizzies* (Impatiens) *look superb in single colours and when mixed. They are ideal in tubs, troughs, windowboxes and hanging baskets.*

• *Grow* Kochia scoparia *'Trichophylla' in a large tub, with colour-contrasting trailing bedding plants around it. Alternatively, plant trailing, variegated, small-leaved ivies around the edges.*

FELICIA bergeriana *(Kingfisher Daisy): Height 15cm/6in, plant 10–15cm/4–6in apart. Mat-forming and bearing grey, hairy leaves and steel-blue flowers with yellow centres from early to late summer.*

IMPATIENS *(Busy Lizzie): Choose dwarf varieties. Height 20–25cm/8–10in, plant 15–20cm/6–8in apart. Flowers in many colours (white, pink, red, scarlet and salmon) from early to late summer.*

KOCHIA scoparia *'Tricophylla' (Burning Bush): Height 60–75cm/2–2 1/2ft, space 30–38cm/12–15in apart. Light green foliage that turns deep red in autumn. 'Childsii' is neater and more compact.*

ANNUALS FOR POTS AND TUBS 3

THE RANGE of annuals that can be grown in containers continues with these summer-flowering beauties. Although the plants discussed on pages 16 to 23 are treated as half-hardy annuals, some are really half-hardy perennials. For example, Scarlet Salvia *(Salvia splendens)*, petunias, the Livingstone Daisy *(Mesembryanthemum criniflorum)* and the Edging Lobelia *(Lobelia erinus)* are perennials that are only half-hardy in temperate and cool climates. In their warm, native countries, however, these plants are fully hardy.

SYPHILITIC CURE

The Blue Cardinal Flower (Lobelia siphilitica) *of North America was introduced into Britain in about 1665. It gained the second part of its botanical name because the Swedish botanist Pehr Kalm, on returning from America, reported that it was being used by the Indians as a remedy for venereal disease. European physicians never confirmed this use.*

RAISING PLANTS

- Edging Lobelia *(Lobelia erinus)*: Sow seeds – barely covering them – from mid-winter to early spring in 15–20°C/59–68°F. Germination takes one to two weeks. When large enough to handle, prick out the seedlings into small clusters in seed-trays. Slowly acclimatize them to outdoor temperatures.
- *Malope trifida*: This is usually sown outdoors and grown as a hardy annual. However, to produce plants for growing in pots and tubs, sow seeds 3mm/$^1/_8$in deep during early spring in 16°C/61°F. Transplant young seedlings into small pots, slowly acclimatize them to outdoor conditions and later plant into containers.

LOBELIA ERINUS *(Edging Lobelia): Height 10–23cm/4–9in, but also trailing: plant 10cm/4in apart. Blue, white or red flowers from late spring to autumn. Trailing varieties soften container edges.*

MALOPE TRIFIDA: *Height 60–75cm/2–2$^1/_2$ft, plant 23cm/9in apart. Bushy, hardy annuals bearing mid-green leaves and trumpet-shaped, 5–7.5cm/2–3in wide, rose-purple flowers, early to late summer.*

MESEMBRYANTHEMUM CRINIFLORUM *(Livingstone Daisy): Height 10–15cm/4–6in: plant 20–25cm/8–10in apart. Spreading, with daisy-like flowers about 2.5cm/1in wide, early to mid-summer.*

NICOTIANA *x* SANDERAE *(Flowering Tobacco Plant): Height 25–50cm/10–20in, plant 15–38cm/6–15in apart. These low-growing forms (others are taller) are superb in pots and tubs.*

PETUNIA *x* HYBRIDA *(Garden Petunia): Height 15–38cm/6–15in, plant 20–30cm/8–12in apart. Trumpet-shaped flowers from early summer to the frosts of autumn. Single and double forms in many colours.*

SALVIA SPLENDENS *(Scarlet Salvia): Height 30–38cm/12–15in, plant 25–30cm/10–12in apart. Usually scarlet flowers. However, there are several other varieties, in purple, salmon and white.*

- Livingstone Daisy *(Mesembryanthemum criniflorum)*: Sow seeds 3mm/1/8in deep from mid-winter to mid-spring in 16–20°C/61–68°F. Germination takes two to three weeks. When large enough to handle, prick off seedlings into small pots, and acclimatize to outdoor conditions.
- Flowering Tobacco Plant *(Nicotiana* x *sanderae)*: Sow seeds 3mm/1/8in deep from late winter to mid-spring in 15–20°C/59–68°F. Germination takes ten to fourteen days. When large enough to handle, prick out the seedlings into seed-trays and acclimatize to outdoor conditions.
- Garden Petunia *(Petunia* x *hybrida)*: Sow seeds thinly on the surface of compost during late winter and early spring in 15–20°C/59–68°F. Germination takes one to two weeks. When large enough to handle, transfer the seedlings into seed-trays and slowly acclimatize to outdoor conditions.
- Scarlet Salvia *(Salvia splendens)*: Sow seeds 6mm/1/4in deep during late winter and early spring in 20°C/68°F. Germination takes two to three weeks. When large enough to handle, transfer the seedlings into seed-trays, harden off and plant into containers as soon as all risk of frost has passed.

MIXING AND MATCHING

- *Scarlet Salvia* (Salvia splendens) *looks superb when combined with white and light blue flowers, as well as silver-leaved plants. In a large tub, combine this variety with Dusty Miller* (Cineraria maritima/ Senecio bicolor).
- *Combine a dark blue, trailing lobelia with a pink Wax Begonia* (Begonia semperflorens).
- *Dark blue, trailing lobelia combines well with pink pelargoniums.*
- *Plant light or dark blue lobelia with French Marigolds* (Tagetes patula). *Both of these are very brightly coloured.*

ANNUALS FOR POTS AND TUBS 4

THE RANGE of annuals continues with the highly floriferous, French and African Marigolds. Select only dwarf types for growing in containers – there are many to choose from.

RAISING PLANTS

- African Marigolds (*Tagetes erecta*): Sow seeds 6mm/1/4in deep during late winter and early spring in 18°C/64°F. Germination takes seven to ten days. When large enough to handle, transfer the seedlings into seed-trays. Slowly acclimatize the plants to outdoor conditions.
- French Marigolds (*Tagetes patula*): Sow seeds in the same way as for African Marigolds.
- *Ursinia anethoides*: Sow seeds 3mm/1/8in deep from late winter to mid-spring in 15°C/59°F. Germination takes ten to fourteen days. When large enough to handle, transfer the seedlings into seed-trays, then slowly acclimatize them to outdoor conditions. Plant into containers as soon as there is no risk of frost.
- Monarch of the Veldt (*Venidium fastuosum*): Sow seeds – lightly covering them – during early and mid-spring in 16°C/61°F. Germination takes two to three weeks. When large enough to handle, prick off the seedlings into small pots. Plant into containers when all risk of frost has passed.

SPACINGS FOR PLANTS

For the plants described on pages 16 to 23, the planting distances suggested are for growing them in containers. To create a colour display quickly, plants are spaced closer than if in a garden. In gardens, increase the recommended spacings by about one-third.

TAGETES ERECTA *(African Marigolds): Height 25–38cm/10–15in, plant 20–25cm/8–10in apart. Dark green leaves and large, daisy-like, lemon-yellow flowers from mid to late summer. Many varieties.*

TAGETES PATULA *(French Marigolds): Height 30–45cm/12–18in, plant 25–30cm/10–12in apart. Dark green leaves and yellow or mahogany-red flowers from early to late summer. Many varieties for tubs.*

URSINIA ANETHOIDES: *Height 23–38cm/9–15in, plant 20–30cm/8–12in apart. Bushy plants with light green leaves and orange, daisy-like flowers with bright orange-yellow centres, from early to late summer.*

• Vervain (*Verbena* x *hybrida*): Sow seeds 3mm/1/8in deep from late winter to early spring in 15–20°C/59–68°F. Germination takes two to three weeks. When growing strongly, prick off the seedlings into seed-trays and slowly acclimatize to outdoor conditions.

• Youth-and-old-age (*Zinnia elegans*): Sow seeds 6mm/1/4in deep during early and mid-spring in 15–20°C/59–68°F. Germination takes ten to fourteen days. When the seedlings are large enough to handle, transfer into seed-trays and slowly acclimatize them to outdoor conditions.

MEXICAN BEAUTY

Known in North America as the Big Marigold, the flowers of the Mexican Tagetes erecta *have been used in India as a source of a yellow dye.* Tagetes lucida, *a native of Central America and Mexico, has flowers that have been used locally as a condiment.*

MIXING AND MATCHING

• *Plant a group of orange-yellow* Ursinia anethoides *on their own in a large tub, then position next to it a dominantly blue-flowered container.*

• *When mixing French or African Marigolds, use fewer of them than other plants. If too many are used, they overwhelm the display.*

• *In large tubs, plant several Dusty Miller* (Cineraria maritima/Senecio bicolor) *surrounded by a collar of low-growing, small-flowered marigolds.*

• *Large tubs planted solely with a colour mixture of zinnias look superb, especially when in full sun. Several containers planted like this and peppered over a patio are certain to introduce vitality. However, do not cluster them together as they will then compete for attention.*

VENIDIUM FASTUOSUM *(Monarch of the Veldt): Height 50–60cm/20–24in, plant 25cm/10in apart. Deeply lobed, woolly leaves and large, orange flowers with black-purple centres.*

VERBENA *x* HYBRIDA *(Vervain): Height 15–38cm/6–15in, plant 15–25cm/6–10in apart. Masses of 7.5cm/3in-wide flower clusters in white, pink, red, blue and lilac from early to late summer.*

ZINNIA ELEGANS *(Youth-and-old-age): Height 15–38cm/6–15in (dwarf strains), plant 15–30cm/6–12in apart. Bright-faced, daisy-like flowers in a wide colour range from mid-summer to autumn frosts.*

TENDER PERENNIALS

GERANIUMS and fuchsias are the best known tender perennials for brightening patios and other areas around houses in summer.

A few fuchsias – the Hardy Fuchsia *(Fuchsia magellanica)* for example – are hardy enough to be left in flower borders throughout the year in temperate regions, but most are frost-tender. In any case, plants growing in pots and left outside during winter are more likely to be damaged by cold temperatures than those planted directly into flower borders, as the compost in pots is more likely to freeze, especially when excessively wet.

PELARGONIUMS *(erroneously known as geraniums) create spectacular displays in pots on patios. They are easily damaged by frost and therefore cannot be left outdoors during winter. Instead, move them into conservatories or frost-proof greenhouses. Proper geraniums are hardy, herbaceous plants.*

PELARGONIUMS

The range of these plants is wide and includes both species types as well as those that have received a great deal of attention from plant breeders. For example, both regal and zonal pelargoniums are hybrids which were raised by crossing species. From these have been derived many distinctive varieties. Both of these types can be grown in pots on sheltered patios during summer.

Do not plant them outdoors until all risk of frost has passed. Regal types, which are not as hardy as zonals, are best increased from cuttings taken in late

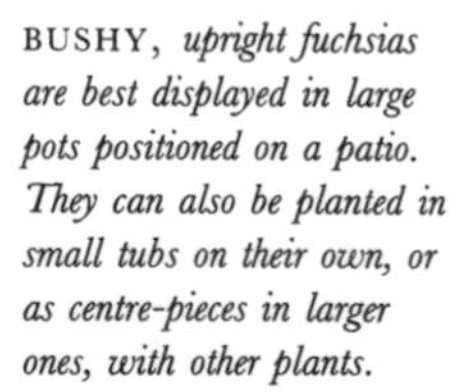

BUSHY, *upright fuchsias are best displayed in large pots positioned on a patio. They can also be planted in small tubs on their own, or as centre-pieces in larger ones, with other plants.*

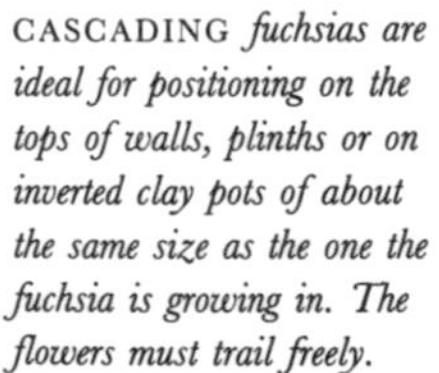

CASCADING *fuchsias are ideal for positioning on the tops of walls, plinths or on inverted clay pots of about the same size as the one the fuchsia is growing in. The flowers must trail freely.*

WALL-BRACKETS *are ideal for small pots planted with trailing and cascading fuchsia varieties. These can look especially good in small groups, rather than as solitary plants.*

TYPES OF FUCHSIA FLOWERS

The range of fuchsia flowers is wide and can be classified in several types: Single (with four petals); Semi-double (having five, six or seven petals); Double (with eight or more petals) and species types, such as Fuchsia magellanica.

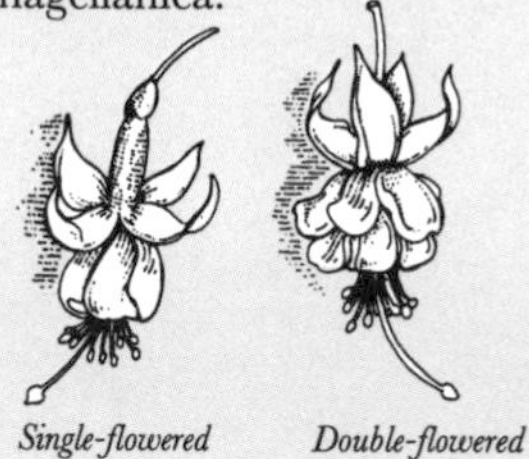

Single-flowered *Double-flowered*

Semi-double *Fuchsia magellanica (Hardy Fuschia)*

summer and overwintered as rooted cuttings. Zonal types (also known as Martha Washington Geraniums) can be overwintered as growing plants in frost-proof greenhouses or conservatories.

GROWING FUCHSIAS

If you buy a tender fuchsia in early summer to plant in a pot or small tub on a patio, when considering what to do with it in late summer you have two choices: leave it until frost kills it, or take it into a frost-proof greenhouse. If the latter, gradually decrease its amount of water, and after the leaves fall, give no more until growth is restarted in spring. Then, plants are trimmed back slightly, watered and given a temperature of 10°C/50°F.

If the roots of plants are congested, repot them into slightly larger pots in early spring. Once plants are growing strongly, feed them every ten days with a weak liquid feed from early to late summer. However, ensure that the fertilizer is not strong, as otherwise it may damage the roots.

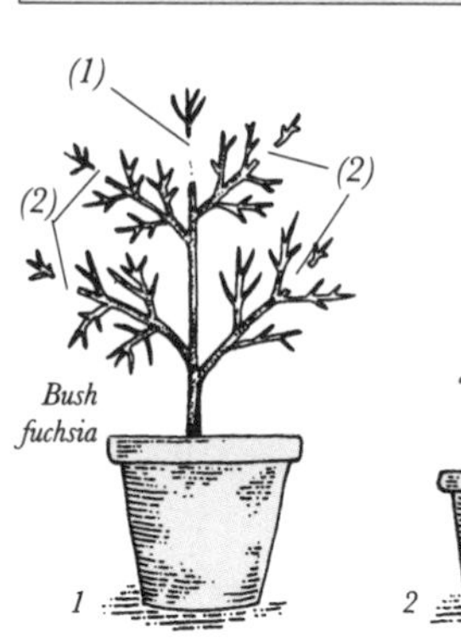

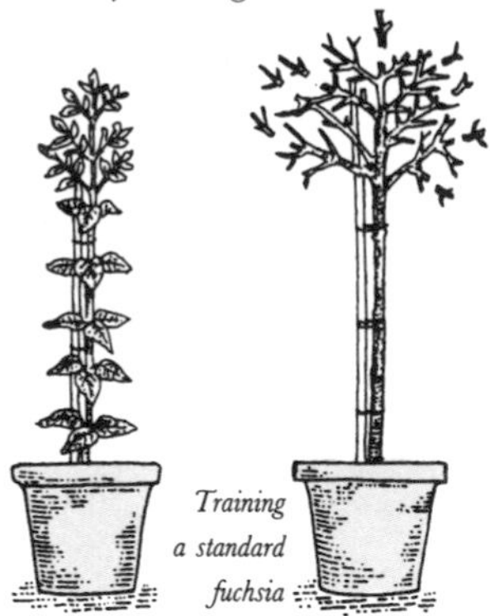

TRAINING *bush fuchsias is relatively easy. First, pinch out the growing tip (1) to encourage the development of sideshoots. When these form, their growing points (2) are also pinched out.*

STANDARD *fuchsias are not difficult to create. Rooted cuttings are grown with their tips removed and trained up canes (1). Remove sideshoots from all but the top three pairs of leaf joints (2).*

REGULARLY *move plants with congested roots into larger pots. When the plant reaches the desired height (see above), remove the growing tip and pinch out the sideshoots (3), as they develop.*

HARDY BORDER PLANTS 1

THESE are plants that can be left in tubs or large pots for several years, until they are congested and need to be removed and divided. They are also border plants. Therefore, where a patio or terrace nestles alongside flower beds, similar plants can be used in tubs and pots to extend the theme and colour pattern.

LOOKING AFTER BORDER PLANTS

The main problem when growing these plants in containers is to keep the compost moist in summer, but relatively dry in winter. Compost rich in peat will help to retain moisture in summer, but should this become dry it is more difficult than soil-based compost to re-moisten. In winter, saturated soil is more likely to freeze and damage roots. Covering the surface with straw helps to keep the compost dry and prevent freezing.

SELECTING PLANTS

In addition to the border plants suggested here and on pages 28 and 29, it is always worth experimenting with others. There are, however, a few guide-lines for this:

- Select relatively low-growing plants, especially if your garden is exposed to wind.
- If the leaves remain throughout winter, choose plants that are dome-headed and create little resistance to wind. Also, they are less likely to be damaged by snow.
- Choose plants that have both interesting flowers and foliage, especially if the flowering period is short. Hostas, of course, have this dual role and several are described on pages 28 and 29.
- Select winter-brightening plants as well as those that reveal their beauty in summer. Winter flowers, as well as frost on large-leaved plants, such as bergenias, dramatically brighten gardens.

AGAPANTHUS CAMPANULATUS *(African Lilies): Height 60–75cm/2–2½ft, spread 38–45cm/15–18in. Herbaceous plant with strap-like leaves and crowded, umbrella-like heads of pale blue flowers in late summer.*

HELLEBORUS ORIENTALIS *(Lenten Rose): Height 45–60cm/1½–2ft, spread 45–50cm/18–20in. Dark green, evergreen leaves and saucer-shaped cream flowers flecked with crimson during late winter and into early spring.*

DICENTRA SPECTABILIS *(Bleeding Heart): Height 45–60cm/1½–2ft, spread 45cm/1½ft. Herbaceous, with grey-green leaves and rosy-red, heart-shaped flowers on arching stems during late spring and early summer.*

ANTHEMIS CUPANIANA: *Height 15–30cm/6–12in, spread 30–38cm/12–15in. Cushion-forming herbaceous perennial. Bright, white, daisy-like flowers with yellow centres during early and mid-summer.*

BERGENIA CORDIFOLIA *(Elephant's Ear): Height 30cm/12in, spread 30–38cm/12–15in. Large, rounded leaves and dominant, clustered heads of bell-shaped, slighty dropping lilac-rose flowers during early and mid-spring.*

SEDUM SPECTABILE: *Height 30–38cm/12–15in, spread 38–45cm/15–18in. Hardy, with a perennial nature and grey-green leaves. Also, clustered heads up to 13cm/5in wide, of pink flowers during late summer and autumn.*

BORDER PLANTS FOR CONTAINERS

Hardy plants feature here and on pages 28 and 29.

- *Aegopodium podagraria* 'Variegata' (Variegated Ground Elder/ Variegated Goutweed): Because it is a relative of the infamous Ground Elder, this needs to be constrained in a tub. Nevertheless, it is exceptionally attractive, with light to mid-green leaves edged in white. It retains its colours even when positioned in light shade. It grows 15–25cm/6–10in high and is increased by division, but do not plant it in a border.
- *Agapanthus* 'Lilliput': A diminutive African Lily with narrow, mid-green leaves and stems topped with bright blue, trumpet-like flowers in umbrella-shaped heads during summer.
- *Dicentra* 'Snowflakes' (Bleeding Heart): Delicately and finely cut mid-green leaves surmounted by clusters of pendulous, white, bee-attracting flowers from early to late summer. It looks better in a large, round pot than in a tub, which may appear to dominate it.

CHRISTMAS ROSES

Helleborus niger, *the well-known Christmas Rose, is associated with in legend and superstition. It is said that people from Gaul – an ancient area that is now northern Italy, France and much of central and northern Europe – rubbed their arrow-heads with hellebore juice before hunting, to make the meat they killed more tender.*

In medieval times it was used to keep away evil spirits and witches, and for breaking enchantments and spells. It was also a cure for cattle that fell ill: a hole was bored through the animal's ear and a piece of hellebore root inserted for twenty-four hours. This was said to effect a cure. It was also said to cure coughs and poisoning.

HARDY BORDER PLANTS 2

THE RANGE of border plants for containers continues, with further ones to consider:

- *Hakonechloa macra* 'Albo-aurea': Although normally grown in a slightly raised bed where it can arch freely, this ornamental grass is also ideal for planting in tubs or large pots, preferably those that are quite tall so that it can cascade unhindered. The graceful, narrow leaves are vividly variegated gold and buff, with touches of bronze. It grows to about 30cm/12in high before cascading.
- *Polygonum affine* 'Dimity': Usually used to carpet borders but equally good in wide, relatively low tubs where it can smother the surface and trail over the edges. The massed, green leaves assume rich autumn shades, while from early to late summer it bears deep pink, poker-like flower heads.
- *Epimedium perralderianum* (Barrenwort/Bishop's Hat): Creeping, mat-forming evergreen plant, often used in borders as ground-cover but also good in large tubs. The bright green leaves, with bronze markings, turn coppery-red in autumn. Sprays of yellow flowers appear in late spring and early summer.
- *Alchemilla mollis* (Lady's Mantle): Beautiful plant, often positioned at the edges of borders where it softens the sides of paths. In large tubs it is just as attractive. The light green, hairy leaves are dominated from early to mid-summer by branched, wispy heads of yellowish-green flowers.

This plant is often used in floral arrangements, but when removing leaves and flowers always cut them from the rear to preserve the plant's appearance.

HOSTA CRISPULA *(Plantain Lily): Height 38–45cm/15–18in, spread 45–50cm/18–20in. Dark green, lance-shaped, pointed leaves with narrow, white edges and lilac-purple flowers during mid-summer.*

HOSTA SIEBOLDIANA *(Plantain Lily): Height 45–60cm/1½–2ft, spread 50–60cm/20–24in. Oval, mid-green, glossy leaves and dull white flowers, tinged purple, during mid-summer. 'Elegans' has lilac flowers.*

FESTUCA GLAUCA *(Sheep's Festuca): Height 20–25cm/8–10in, spread 20–25cm/8–10in. Hardy, perennial, ornamental grass with bluish-grey, bristle-like leaves that eventually form a large tuft.*

STACHYS OLYMPICA/ Stachys byzantina *(Lamb's Tongue): Height 30–38cm/12–15in, spread 38–45cm/15–18in. Spreading herbaceous perennial with oval leaves smothered in soft, furry silvery hairs.*

PHORMIUM TENAX *(New Zealand Flax): Height 90cm–1.2m/3–4ft, spread 90–1.2m/3–4ft. Masses of tall, sword-like leaves. Many superb varieties, some variegated, others just one colour. Protect crowns in winter from excessive water.*

HEBE *x* ANDERSONII *'Variegata' (Shrubby Veronica): Height 45–60cm/1½–2ft, spread 45–60cm/1½–2ft. Shrubby, tender perennial bearing beautiful mid-green leaves variegated with cream. Lavender flowers in summer.*

FUNKIA OR HOSTA?

Even until quite recently, many gardeners still called hostas by their old name, funkia. Commonly, they are known as Plantain Lilies. Some of them grow 1m/3½ft or more high, but it is the lower ones that make superb displays in large pots and tubs. In recent years, plant hybridists in North America, Japan and Britain have given these plants much attention, creating richer coloured leaves and a more dwarfed stance. Hostas for containers include:

- Hosta *'Blue Moon': A superb, small-leaved hybrid with deep blue leaves and thickish clusters of greyish-mauve flowers.*
- Hosta crispula: *see left.*
- Hosta *'Golden Prayers': Golden-yellow leaves and mauve flowers.*
- Hosta *'Shade Fanfare': Green leaves with broad, cream edges. The green turns yellow when in sunlight.*
- Hosta sieboldiana: *see left.*
- Hosta *'Thomas Hogg': Rich green, flat leaves with broad, white edges.*
- Hosta *'Wide Brim': An American variety, with oval, blue-green leaves irregularly edged in cream to golden-yellow. It also bears spikes of lavender-coloured flowers.*
- Hosta *'Zounds': Large, oval, dominant, deeply-puckered, yellow leaves.*

TREES AND SHRUBS

TREES, shrubs and conifers introduce permanency to patios. They can be displayed on their own or in groups. Their range of sizes and shapes is wide and there are sure to be many for you to choose from. Some develop flowers (pages 32 and 33), while others have beautiful foliage (pages 34 and 35). Small conifers are featured on pages 38 and 39.

EXOTIC PATIOS

If your garden is warm, sunny and sheltered during summer, consider creating an exotic patio or courtyard, using slightly tender plants. Of course it is necessary to take them into a frost-free greenhouse or conservatory during winter, but their effect on a patio can be dramatic and memorable – and certainly will surprise and impress neighbours and visitors. Some of these plants, especially those in small pots, can also be put indoors in cool but bright hallways and other rooms during winter.

Popular plants include:

- *Agave americana* 'Marginata' (Variegated Century Plant): Height 45–60cm/1½–2ft. Large, thick and succulent, sword-like, grey-green leaves with yellow edges. The ordinary type just has grey-green leaves, but nevertheless is ideal in a group as a foil for variegated plants.
- *Cordyline australis/Dracaena australis* (Cabbage Palm): Eventually tall and shrubby, but in pots in homes and on patios is seldom more than 90cm/3ft high. The narrow, spiky, grey-green leaves rise from a stiff, upright, central stem. In warm, mild areas outdoors, plants more than ten years old may develop plumes of fragrant, creamy-white flowers during early and mid-summer.

COURTYARDS *need one or two large, evergreen shrubs to form focal points and to help camouflage bland walls. If a courtyard is large, they also fill large areas and create fixed points, around which plants in small pots can be grouped.*

FLATS *and apartment blocks often have paved areas around them. These are easily brightened by shrubs and trees in large tubs. These plants can be given some protection from people by positioning them on uneven, cobbled surfaces.*

ULTRA-MODERN *patios, formed of brightly-coloured, square or hexagonal paving slabs need clinical-looking plants to compliment them. Spiky yuccas are ideal for this, especially when planted in geometric, square-edged, formal containers.*

- *Trachycarpus fortunei/Chamaerops excelsa* (Chusan Palm/Fan Palm): Evergreen palm, only sufficiently hardy to be planted outside in warm areas. But in a pot, it can – while still small – be given sojourns on sheltered patios in summer. The large, pleated fans are often 90cm/3ft wide, while eventually the trunk develops attractive black, wiry fibres.
- *Phoenix canariensis* (Canary Island Date Palm): In its native country it grows 4.5m/15ft or more high, but in a pot and when young is often grown as a houseplant. In warm areas, place it outdoors in summer. The slender leaves arch outwards, with stiff, mid-green leaflets attached to them.
- Yucca: Several yuccas, such as *Yucca filamentosa*, *Y. gloriosa* and *Y. recurvifolia* are relatively hardy, even in temperate zones. These look superb and exotic in tubs on patios, while some of the tender ones like *Y. elephantipes* (Spineless Yucca) and *Y. aloifolia* (Spanish Bayonet) can be placed outdoors during warm summer days. Take care with spiny plants not to position them where they may be a danger to children.

The variegated forms of *Yucca filamentosa* are exceptionally attractive: 'Variegata' has green leaves with creamy-yellow stripes, while 'Golden Sword' reveals upright, yellow leaves, shaped like swords and edged in green.

BUYING SHRUBS AND TREES

Buying all plants needs care, but trees and shrubs require special attention, as they will be with you for many years. Always check that the foliage is not damaged or infested with pests or diseases. Also, the compost must be slightly moist and not covered with moss or algae, which would indicate that the plant had been in the container too long and that the roots may be constricted.

RUSTIC *settings demand gently rounded and irregular outlines from a mixture of flowering and foliaged shrubs and trees. Create informal groups, such as shrubs in tubs and old stone sinks on brick piers, rather than isolated plants.*

ENCLOSED *patios create wind sheltered areas, often warm and drenched in sun. These are ideal for tender, shrubby plants that elsewhere would not be successful. In such areas, daily watering is essential, especially at the height of summer.*

ROOF *gardens create exciting gardening opportunities, but too frequently are buffeted by cold winds in winter and 'fried' by strong sunlight in summer. Therefore, erect screens and windbreaks to create shelter and protection.*

FLOWERING SHRUBS

MANY flowering shrubs can be grown in containers, from dominant camellias at 1.5–1.8m/5–6ft high to tub-hugging types such as ericas. In addition to the ones illustrated on these pages, others to consider include the following:

- *Camellia* x *williamsii* (Camellia): Height 1.5–1.8m/5–6ft – in a large tub, spread 1.2–1.5m/4–5ft. Wide range of varieties, in colours from white and pale pink to rose-purple. Flowering is mainly in late winter and spring. Position out of direct, early-morning sun.
- *Genista pilosa* 'Vancouver Gold' (Broom): Height 15–30cm/6–12in, spread 90cm–1.2m/3–4ft. Compact, evergreen shrub with masses of deep golden-yellow flowers during late spring and early summer.
- *Prunus incisa* 'Kojo Nomal' (Flowering Cherry): Height 1.2–1.4m/4–5ft, spread 90cm–1.2m/3–4ft. A beautiful, deciduous flowering cherry that will delight you throughout the year: red-centred, pink flowers in spring that fade to white; colourful leaves in autumn; and twiggy, branching stems in winter.
- *Clematis florida sieboldii:* Height 1.5–1.8m, spread 75–90cm/2½–3ft. Bushy, mid-summer-flowering climber that is ideal in large pots. The large flowers, resembling those of the Passion Flower, have white petals and violet-purple petal-like stamens. Provide it with long twiggy sticks as supports.
- Roses: Several varieties within the perpetual-flowering County Series of roses grow well in containers on a patio. Those especially suited include 'Hertfordshire', with single, carmine flowers on a

HYPERICUM *'Hidcote': Height 90cm–1.2m/3–4ft, spread 90cm–1.2m/3–4ft. Hardy, evergreen shrub with large, dark green leaves and shallow saucer-shaped, golden-yellow flowers, up to 6cm/2½in wide, from mid to late summer.*

HYPERICUM OLYMPICUM: *Height 20–30cm/8–12in, spread 30–38cm/12–15in. Low-growing, hardy, evergreen shrub with grey-green leaves and golden-yellow flowers up to 36mm/1½in wide during mid-summer.*

LAVANDULA *'Hidcote'*/L. nana atropurpurea *(Lavender): Height 30–50cm/12–20in, spread 45–60cm/18–24in. Dwarf, hardy, evergreen shrub with silvery leaves and deep purple-blue flowers from mid to late summer.*

EVERGREEN AZALEAS *(Japanese Azaleas): Height 45–60cm/1½–2ft, spread 60–75cm/2–2½ft. Evergreen shrubs, some slightly tender, with flowers in massed heads during spring. Many colours.*

RHODODENDRONS: *Choose varieties no more than 1.5m/5ft high and broad. Wide range of varieties and colours, including red, pink, white, lavender and yellow. Flowers mainly in late spring.*

ROSMARINUS OFFICINALIS *(Rosemary): Normally 1.8m/6ft high, but if grown in a large tub and the growing points are pinched out several times, it can be kept to 1.2m/4ft high. Flowers all summer.*

low spreading shrub during summer. 'Suffolk' is also spreading, with bright scarlet, single flowers with golden centres.

Patio and miniature roses can also be grown in tubs and pots.

- *Convolvulus cneorum*: Height 45–60cm/1½–2ft, spread 45–60cm/1½–2ft. Compact, bushy, half-hardy evergreen shrub bearing narrow leaves covered with silky, silvery hairs. From late spring to late summer it develops pink buds that open to reveal white flowers.
- *Erica herbacea/Erica carnea* (Snow Heather/Spring Heather): Height 10–30cm/4–12in, spread 30–45cm/1–1½ft. Wide range of varieties in various heights. The flowers are white and shades of pink and red from late autumn to late spring. For extra colour, choose those varieties with coloured foliage as they create colour throughout the year.
- *Mahonia* 'Charity': Height 1.5–1.8m/5–6ft, spread 90cm–1.6m/3–6ft. A tall, eye-catching shrub that eventually has to be removed from its container and planted into a woodland or wild garden setting. The large, holly-like, dark green leaflets are surmounted from late autumn to late winter by arching spires of fragrant, deep yellow flowers. Position it in sun or light shade, and away from where the sharp leaves can hurt children.

MOP-HEAD *Hydrangeas* (Hydrangea macrophylla) *are superb on patios, terraces and verandahs, where they blanket containers with large flower heads (mainly blue or pink) from mid to late summer.*

ATTRACTIVE FOLIAGE

SHRUBS with attractive foliage introduce colour and vitality to patios and terraces throughout summer. Evergreen shrubs continue their display throughout winter, while the leaves of deciduous types often create a burst of exceptionally bright colour before falling in autumn. The range of attractively foliaged shrubs is wide:

- *Berberis thunbergii* 'Aurea': Height 60–75cm/2–2½ft, spread 60–75cm/2–2½ft. Deciduous shrub with masses of small, bright, soft-yellow leaves. There are several other superb forms, including 'Atropurpurea' (rich purple-red leaves), 'Atropurpurea Nana' (dwarf form with rich, purple-red leaves) and 'Helmond Pillar' (dark purple leaves).
- *Calluna vulgaris* (Heather/Ling): Height 15–30cm/6–12in (range of varieties), spread 30–38cm/12–15in. Hardy, evergreen shrub. There are many attractively foliaged varieties, including 'Gold Haze' (bright gold), 'Golden Carpet' (golden foliage flecked with orange and red during winter), 'Beoley Gold' (golden) and 'Blazeaway' (foliage changes from gold, through orange to red).
- *Choisya ternata* 'Sundance' (Yellow-leaved Mexican Orange Blossom): Height 75–90cm/2½–3ft, spread 75–90cm/2½–3ft. Golden leaves throughout the year, with the bonus of white, scented flowers in spring.
- *Elaeagnus pungens* 'Maculata': Height 1.5–2.1m/5–7ft, spread 1.5–1.8m/5–6ft. Evergreen, spiny-stemmed shrub bearing leathery, glossy green leaves splashed with gold. Eventually it becomes too large for tubs, when it can be planted into gardens.
- *Euonymus fortunei* 'Emerald 'n Gold': Height 45–60cm/1½–2ft,

HEBE *x* FRANCISCANA *'Variegata': Height 30–45cm/12–18in, spread 30–45cm/12–18in. Dome shaped, compact shrub with glossy green leaves edged in cream, and mauve-blue flowers throughout summer.*

FATSIA JAPONICA *(False Castor Oil Plant): Height 1.5–2.1m/5–7ft, spread 1.5–1.8m/5–6ft. Slightly tender shrub, with large, glossy, hand-like, coarsely edged leaves and white flowers in late summer and autumn.*

AUCUBA JAPONICA *'Maculata' (Spotted Laurel): Height 1.5–1.8m/5–6ft, spread 1.2–1.5m/4–5ft. Dome shaped, evergreen shrub bearing glossy green leaves peppered with yellow spots. Also known as 'Variegata'.*

ACER PALMATUM *'Dissectum Atropurureum': Height 90cm/1.2m/3–4ft, spread 1.2–1.5m/4–5ft. Beautiful deciduous shrub with bronze-red, several-lobed leaves.*

YUCCA FILAMENTOSA *'Variegata': Height 60–75cm/2–2½ft, spread 60cm/2ft. Spiky plant with stiff, mid-green leaves edged and striped in creamy yellow.*

ARUNDINARIA VIRIDISTRIATA: *Height 90cm–1.2m/3–4ft, spread 30–45cm/1–1½ft (clump-forming). Purplish-green canes and green leaves striped yellow.*

spread 60–75cm/2–2½ft. Gloriously coloured evergreen shrub with green, gold and pink leaves. There are several other forms with colourful leaves, including 'Emerald Gaiety' (creamy-white and green leaves).

• *Hebe x andersonii* 'Variegata': Height 60–75cm/2–2½ft, spread 45–60cm/1½–2ft. Small, evergreen shrub with mid-green leaves variegated in cream. Additionally, from mid to late summer it bears spikes of lavender flowers.

• *Hebe pinguifolia* 'Pagei': Height 15–23cm/6–9in, spread 38–45cm/15–18in. Low-growing, evergreen shrub with small, grey leaves. During early summer it has the bonus of small, white flowers borne in spikes up to 2.5cm/1in long.

• *Lonicera nitida* 'Baggeson's Gold': Height 1.2–1.5m/4–5ft, spread 90cm–1.2m/3–4ft (in a tub): Hardy, evergreen shrub with small, yellow leaves that turn yellowish green in autumn. It is often clipped – especially when grown as a hedge – but in a large tub is best left with an informal outline.

• *Sambucus racemosa* 'Sutherland': Height 1.8–2.1m/6–7ft, spread 1.8–2.4m/6–8ft. Spectacular deciduous shrub with finely cut, golden-yellow leaves. Eventually it forms a handsome, much larger shrub, but when young can be grown in a big tub.

TOPIARY IN CONTAINERS

*Large tubs on patios allow an opportunity to train small-leaved evergreen shrubs, such as the Small-leaved Box (*Buxus sempervirens *'Suffruticosa'), into the shape of a small animal. Allow clusters of stems to form the head and tail – wire is usually necessary to create a framework. Pinch out the tips of shoots to ensure bushiness.*

CLIMBERS IN CONTAINERS

CLIMBERS introduce a new dimension to containers on a patio: some of them have a perennial nature and each year send up fresh shoots, while others are raised annually from seeds. Some of the annual types are really tender perennials that are grown as half-hardy annuals. Cathedral Bells (*Cobaea scandens*), for example, is only half-hardy in temperate climates and therefore grown as a half-hardy annual, although in greenhouses and conservatories it can be grown as a permanent, perennial climber.

ANNUAL CLIMBERS

Apart from the seed-raised climbers illustrated here, there are a few others, including:

- Chilean Glory Flower (*Eccrocarpus scaber*): Height 1.5–2.1m/5–7ft (in a container). From early summer to autumn it bears 2.5cm/1in-long, orange-scarlet, tubular flowers. Also has red and yellow forms. Sow seeds in 55–61°C/13–16°F during early spring. Transfer the seedlings to pots, slowly acclimatize to outdoor conditions and plant into a container when all risk of frost has passed.
- Black-eyed Susan (*Thunbergia alata*): Height 1.2–1.8m/4–6ft (in a pot). From early to late summer it bears large, yellow flowers with

SOUTH AMERICAN INFLUENCE

We have South America to thank for the wide range of tropaeolums that today adorn gardens worldwide. Nasturtiums, now available in a vast colour and height range, were the first tropaeolums to reach Europe, initially to Spain and thence to France and Flanders. In Britain they became known as Yellow Larkes Spurr.

CLEMATIS: *Large-flowered types. Height 1.5–1.8m/5–6ft (in tubs). Deciduous climbers with many to choose from. Flowers from early to late summer, depending on the variety. Wide colour range.*

IPOMOEA TRICOLOR/ I. violacea/I. rubro-caerulea *(Morning Glory): Height 1.5–1.8m/5–6ft (in a pot). It is grown as a half-hardy annual, with seed sown in 18°C/64°F in early spring.*

TROPAEOLUM MAJUS *(Nasturtiums): Height 38–45cm/15–18in – dwarf varieties. For planting in pots it is grown as a half-hardy annual. Sow seeds in 16°C/61°F in early spring. Flowers throughout summer.*

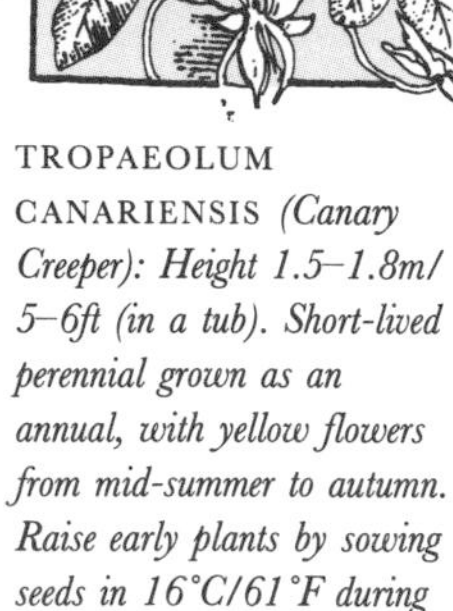

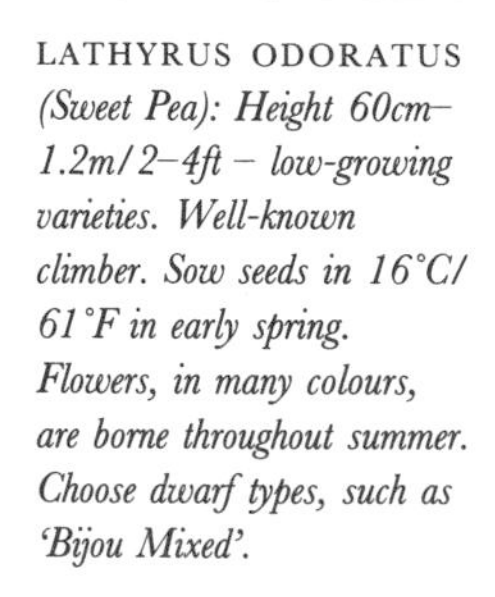

LATHYRUS ODORATUS *(Sweet Pea): Height 60cm–1.2m/2–4ft – low-growing varieties. Well-known climber. Sow seeds in 16°C/61°F in early spring. Flowers, in many colours, are borne throughout summer. Choose dwarf types, such as 'Bijou Mixed'.*

COBAEA SCANDENS *(Cathedral Bells): Height 1.5–1.8m/5–6ft (when grown outdoors). A tender perennial with purple, bell-shaped flowers throughout summer. Grow as a half-hardy annual outdoors. Sow seeds in 16°C/61°F during early spring.*

TROPAEOLUM CANARIENSIS *(Canary Creeper): Height 1.5–1.8m/5–6ft (in a tub). Short-lived perennial grown as an annual, with yellow flowers from mid-summer to autumn. Raise early plants by sowing seeds in 16°C/61°F during early spring.*

dark centres. Sow seeds in 16°C/61°F in early spring. Prick off the seedlings into small pots and plant into containers when all risk of frost has passed.

PERENNIAL CLIMBERS

Apart from perennial climbers such as large-flowered clematis in tubs, the herbaceous Yellow-Leaved Hop (*Humulus lupulus* 'Aureus') is worth growing. It dies down to soil level in autumn, but each spring sends up beautiful, large leaves that remain soft yellow throughout summer. In gardens it grows 2.1m/7ft or more in a season, but in a tub is more reserved. Do not allow the compost to dry out.

Wisteria is usually grown against a wall, although sometimes trained as a single stem to produce a canopy at head height. However, it can also be grown in a large tub or terracotta pot, where it creates an eye-catching display during late spring and early summer.

COLOUR HARMONIES

Matching plants to containers further enhances the display: Nasturtiums harmonize with the earthy look of clay pots, while clematis needs something more ornate to blend with the large, delicate flowers. White-painted tubs contrast well with Morning Glory and Cathedral Bells. The bushy climber and trailer Clematis macropetala *has light and dark blue flowers that create a spectacular display when planted in a large, terracotta pot, especially one that is well weathered.*

Clematis macropetala

CONIFERS

DWARF and slow-growing conifers are easy to grow, as well as representing excellent value for money. They last a long time and if eventually too large for tubs and pots can be planted into a garden. In addition to the conifers illustrated here, there are many others to choose from:

- *Chamaecyparis lawsoniana* 'Aurea Densa': Compact and slow growing, with densely packed sprays of golden foliage.
- *Chamaecyparis lawsoniana* 'Minima Aurea': Dwarf, with vertical, soft golden-yellow sprays that form a conical bush.
- *Chamaecyparis pisifera* 'Boulevard': Soft, steel-blue foliage. Do not allow the soil to become dry.
- *Chamaecyparis pisifera* 'Filifera Aurea': Graceful and rounded with golden, thread-like foliage that eventually forms a mop-headed plant.
- *Cryptomeria japonica* 'Elegans Compacta': Slow growing and dome shaped. Tinged purple in winter.

POSITIONING CONIFERS

One of the biggest dangers to conifers – apart from letting the compost become too dry in summer or excessively wet in winter – is strong winds. Tall plants are soon knocked over and unless put upright immediately may be permanently damaged. In exposed positions, use low-growing types in tubs or heavy, reconstituted stone pots.

JUNIPERUS COMMUNIS *'Depressa Aurea': Dwarf and slow growing with a spreading and low nature, up to 38cm/15in-high and 1–1.2m/3–4ft wide. Golden-yellow leaves, silver beneath. It is especially bright in spring.*

CHAMAECYPARIS LAWSONIANA *'Elwoodii': Slow growing and eventually 1.8m/6ft tall, but when young is ideal for pots and tubs. It is column-like and packed with dark green foliage. 'Ellwood's Golden Pillar' has golden-yellow foliage.*

JUNIPERUS HORIZONTALIS *'Wiltonii' (Wilton Carpet Juniper): Slow growing and carpet forming (15–20cm/6–8in high) and spreading to about 1m/3½ft in six years. Bright blue, dense foliage. Plant it in a large tub with space to spread.*

JUNIPERUS SCOPULORUM *'Skyrocket'/Juniperus virginiana 'Skyrocket': Narrow, upright, slow-growing conifer, about 1.8m/6ft high after ten years. Silvery blue-green, scale-like foliage.*

JUNIPERUS SQUAMATA *'Meyeri': Irregularly shaped, with arching and ascending branches. After about ten years it forms a bush about 1.5m/5ft high. Steel-blue, needle-like leaves. If it spreads excessively, it can be pruned.*

TAXUS BACCATA *'Standishii': Narrow, columnar, slow-growing conifer, reaching only 75cm/ 2½ft in ten years. The old-gold foliage is especially attractive in winter and forms a tight column. It is tolerant of light shade.*

- *Juniperus communis* 'Hibernica': Eventually large, but suitable for tubs when young. Narrow and column-like.
- *Juniperus* x *media* 'Old Gold': Spreading, eventually large but ideal for containers when young. Golden, scale-like foliage.
- *Juniperus squamata* 'Blue Star': Small, low conifer with intense steel-blue, needle-like leaves.
- *Pinus sylvestris* 'Beuvronensis': Distinctive, miniature Scots Pine creating a dome shape packed with grey-green foliage. Especially attractive in spring, when new growth is beginning.
- *Thuja occidentalis* 'Smaragd': Slow-growing, pyramidal and packed with bright, rich green foliage. It retains an attractive colour throughout winter.
- *Thuja plicata* 'Stoneham Gold': Slow growing and ideal in a small tub. The foliage is tipped in deep, golden-yellow.

MINIATURE *and slow-growing conifers create colour in pots, tubs and troughs throughout the year. When planted in a trough which is to be set in a central position, create a 'balanced' display. But when positioned with one end in a corner, create a slanting arrangement.*

SINK GARDENS

IF YOU do not have space for a rock garden or scree bed, form a miniature alpine garden in an old stone sink. There is a wide choice of suitable plants and some of these are illustrated on the opposite page. In addition, miniature conifers are useful to create height at the backs of sinks. Miniature bulbs can also be used. Trailing plants that cascade over the sink's sides are also useful to ensure that upright plants merge with the sink and do not look as if they are just icing on a cake.

CHIMNEY POTS

Unusual containers introduce originality to patios and terraces. Ensure water can drain from them, fill with equal parts compost, peat and coarse grit, then plant with trailing rock garden plants. Alternatively, in summer put pots of hardy, trailing house plants in their tops, such as Strawberry Geranium (Saxifraga stolonifera *'Tricolor'*). *If in an entrance lobby or conservatory, use the Spider Plant* (Chlorophytum comosum *'Variegatum'*).

PLANTING A STONE SINK
First, thoroughly scrub the sink. Then, stand it on four strong housebricks, with a slight slope towards the drainage hole. If the container is placed directly on the ground, slugs and snails can easily attack the plants.

Place crocks or pieces of clay pots over the plug hole, then a 2.5cm/1in layer of 6mm/1/4in pea shingle. Over this, form a 2.5–4cm/1–1 1/2in layer of moist peat. If a deep, glazed sink is being used, double these thicknesses. The compost needed depends on the plants, but for most a mixture of soil-based potting compost with extra peat and sharp sand is suitable. If lime-hating plants are being grown, omit the chalk from the compost or buy a loam-based potting mixture specially for acid-loving plants. Fill and firm the compost to about half the sink's depth, then set a few rocks in position, creating a natural strata by sloping them backwards. Add further compost and put in plants with relatively large root-balls.

Alpine plants are invariably sold in small pots and therefore disturbance to their roots is minimal. Put cushion-forming plants around rocks, with trailing types at the sides. When planting is complete, leave the soil about 2.5cm/1in below the sink's rim. This will allow for a covering of pea shingle or rock chippings, and still leave a 12mm/1/2in space be-tween the soil level and the sink's rim. The compost will sink slightly, so be prepared to add further shingle or chippings.

Planting is usually carried out in autumn, so that plants are well established by spring. In cold, wet areas, leave planting until spring.

ANTENNARIA DIOICA *'Rosea': Deep pink flowers during late spring and early summer.*

CAMPANULA COCHLEARIIFOLIA *(Fairies' Thimbles): Blue bells from mid to late summer.*

ERINUS ALPINUS: *Bright pink, starry flowers from early spring to mid-summer.*

ANDROSACE PRIMULOIDES *'Chumbyi' (Rock Jasmine): Deep rose flowers during spring and early summer.*

LEWISIA COTYLEDON: *Pink flowers with white veins during late spring and early summer.*

SAXIFRAGA BURSERIANA: *Pure white flowers during late winter and early spring.*

EDRAIANTHUS PUMILIO *(Grassy Bells): Lavender-blue flowers from early to mid-summer.*

HEBE BUCHANANII *'Minor': White flowers during early summer.*

BULBS ON PATIOS

FOR AN assured display of colour in containers on a patio, few plants compare with bulbs. They are storehouses of energy and if healthy, fresh bulbs are planted at the right time (invariably in late summer or autumn for a spring display) a feast of colour is assured. In addition to the bulbs illustrated here, there are many others, including:

• *Anemone blanda* (Windflower): Height: 10–15cm/4–6in. Daisy-like flowers – mainly mid-blue, but pale blue, mauve, pink and mauve forms available – from late winter to mid-spring. Plant them 3.6–5mm/1$^1/_2$–2in deep in late summer. They are best when planted around shrubs in large tubs, where they can be left for several years.

• *Crocus chrysanthus*: Height 7.5cm/3in. Globe-shaped flowers in many colours, including golden-yellow, bronze, mauve-blue, white

SCENTED LILIES IN POTS

Lilies introduce dignity and history to patios – they were represented on Cretan vases about 1750 BC. There are several sweetly-scented lilies that can be grown in pots, including:

• Lilium auratum *(Golden-rayed Lily of Japan): Bowl-shaped and brilliant white, with golden-yellow bands, flowering in late summer.*

• Lilium *'Empress of China': Chalk-white, mid to late summer.*

• Lilium hansonii: *Nodding, pale orange-yellow with brown spots during mid-summer.*

• Lilium speciosum: *Bowl-shaped, white and shaded crimson during late summer. There are also several named varieties, in white and shades of crimson.*

MUSCARI ARMENIACUM *(Grape Hyacinth): Height 15–20cm/ 6–8in. Spring-flowering, with clustered heads of deep blue flowers. Plant bulbs 6–7.5cm/ 2$^1/_2$–3in deep and slightly apart in autumn.*

TRUMPET DAFFODILS: *Large height range, but choose low varieties as they are less likely to be damaged by wind. Plant bulbs close together in autumn, so that they are covered by twice their depth of compost. Set them close together.*

TULIPS – *single early types: select short types. Many varieties to choose from: always buy fresh bulbs. Plant bulbs deeply, about three times their own depth and close together, in autumn. They can be mixed with hyacinths.*

HYACINTHS: *Height 15–23cm/6–9in. Upright and soldier-like flowers in many colours, including white, pink and blue. Plant bulbs 13–15cm/5–6in deep and 5–7.5cm/2–3in apart in autumn. Always plant fresh, healthy bulbs.*

NARCISSUS CYCLAMINEUS: *Height 15–20cm/6–8in. A diminutive bulb, flowering in late winter and early spring with golden flowers. Plant bulbs in autumn, 2.5cm/1in apart and two to three times their own depth.*

TULIPA KAUFMANNIANA *(Waterlily Tulip): Height 20–25cm/8–10in. Large, white flowers flushed yellow and red in early and mid-spring. Plant bulbs in autumn, three times their depth and 7.5cm/3in apart.*

and deep purple, during late winter and early spring. Plant them 5–7.5cm/2–3in deep in late summer or autumn.

• *Eranthis hyemalis* (Winter Aconite): Height 10cm/4in. Unusual flowers, with yellow bowls and pale green ruffs at their backs during late winter and early spring. Plant them 2.5cm/1in deep and 6cm/2½in apart in late summer. They look good in clumps around deciduous shrubs in large tubs.

• *Iris danfordiae:* Height 10cm/4in. Diminutive, with honey-scented, bright yellow flowers during mid and late winter. Ideal for planting in sink gardens to create early colour. Plant 5–7.5cm/2–3in deep in autumn. They can be left in the container for several years.

• *Iris reticulata:* Height 10–15cm/4–6in. Beautiful, 6–7.5cm/2½–3in wide, deep blue, iris-like flowers with golden-yellow blazes on the insides of the lower petals. They are ideal for brightening sink gardens, pots and window-boxes in late winter and early spring. Plant them 5–7.5cm/2–3in deep in autumn. Once these bulbs are established they can be left alone for several years.

• *Narcissus bulbocodium* (Yellow Hoop Petticoat): 10–15cm/4–6in. Diminutive, with dainty but long, yellow trumpets. They appear in late winter and early spring. Plant to twice the bulb's depth, and close together. It is ideal for planting in sink gardens.

BULBS IN GROWING-BAGS

Growing-bags that during the previous season grew tomatoes or other vegetable plants can be reused for bulbs. Just top up the bag with moist peat in autumn and set the bulbs in position. Choose short-stemmed types.

VEGETABLES IN CONTAINERS

MANY vegetables can be grown in containers, enabling garden-fresh food to be eaten throughout the summer. However, only vegetables with fibrous or shallow roots are suitable. These include not only those illustrated here, but short-rooted carrots, radishes and French and climbing beans.

- Carrots: Choose short-rooted varieties and sow seeds 12mm/ $^1/_2$in deep from mid-spring to mid-summer, in drills about 13cm/5in apart. Later, thin the seedlings to about 36–50mm/ $1^1/_2$–2in apart.
- Dwarf beans (Bush type): These can be grown in pots as well as growing-bags. Sow twelve seeds 36mm/$1^1/_2$in deep in a standard-sized growing-bag during late spring or early summer, as soon as all risk of frost has passed. Water the compost gently. Pick the beans when young to encourage more to grow. Ensure that the compost is moisture-retentive.

SEAKALE POTS

Seakale has been forced for several centuries and in 1860 the magazine Profitable Gardening *illustrated Pascall's Patent Sea-Kale Pot for forcing seakale indoors. The lower pot held well-drained compost, while the upper pot (which rested in a small ledge) created a dark and slightly warm chamber.*

EARLY *potatoes: In early spring, plant four or five seed potatoes on a 7.5cm/3in layer of compost and put 10–13cm/4–5in over them. Cover shoots with layers of compost to within 36mm/ $1^1/_2$in of the rim. Harvest three months later.*

LETTUCES: *These are ideal for planting in growing-bags, as well as large boxes. Sow seeds 12mm/ $^1/_2$in deep in ten to twelve groups of three seeds in a standard growing-bag in spring. Later, remove the weakest seedlings.*

TOMATOES: *Popular plants for growing in pots on warm patios. When all risk of frost has passed, plant established plants into pots. Support with canes, remove sideshoots and pinch out growing tips two leaves above the fourth truss.*

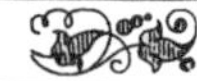

AUBERGINES *(Egg Plants): Put three established plants in a growing-bag when all risk of frost has passed. When 30cm/12in high, pinch out the growing tips. Feed plants every two weeks and pick fruits when 10–20cm/4–8in long.*

BEETROOT: *They normally need deep soil, so choose baby or globe types and grow in growing-bags or large pots. Sow seeds thinly and evenly, 18mm/3/4in deep, from mid-spring to early summer. Harvest roots when young.*

SWEET PEPPERS: *Ideal for growing-bags. When all risk of frost has passed, put three young plants in a growing-bag. When they are 15cm/ 6in high, pinch out their growing tips. Support and feed every two weeks. Harvest in late summer.*

• Climbing beans: These are quite at home in growing-bags, but they must be supported. Success – as with all beans – relies on plenty of moisture at the roots of plants and an abundance of sun on their leaves. Position the bags against a warm, sun-drenched wall and water well before adding plants. Although seeds can be sown, it is quicker to buy established young plants and to plant them as soon as all risk of frost has passed – about late spring or early summer.

Put ten plants in a standard growing-bag, or six in a mini-sized one. Keep the compost moist, but not waterlogged, and provide supports (see right). Pick the beans while young to encourage the development of others.

• Radishes: These are popular and quick to mature. Sow in either growing-bags, troughs or wooden boxes, 12mm/1/2in deep from mid-spring to mid-summer. Sow thinly and harvest the bulbous roots while still young.

SUPPORTING PLANTS IN GROWING-BAGS

When growing plants such as tomatoes and climbing beans in growing-bags it is essential to support them. Because stakes cannot normally be pushed into growing-bags, a self-supporting framework is essential. Proprietary metal types are available (see below), but home-made ones are easily constructed from wood, or stakes and wire.

HERBS IN POTS

NO PATIO is complete without a few pots of herbs nestling near a kitchen door. Apart from saving journeys into the garden, groups of herbs are very decorative. Some have attractive flowers, but all have decorative leaves that soon enrich paved areas. Additionally, once you have established herbs, most are easily increased by division, cuttings or sowing seeds and therefore continuing your supply becomes quite inexpensive.

RANGE OF HERBS

The best herbs for containers are low-growing types: tall ones are soon bent and damaged, or in wind-exposed positions, pots are knocked over. Fortunately, this does not exclude some of the best and most widely used herbs. Some of these are illustrated on these pages, but others include:

- Balm (*Melissa officinalis*): A hardy herbaceous perennial that normally forms a mound 60cm–1.2m/2–4ft high, but in a tub is restrained and only 45–60cm/1½–2ft. It is bushy, with pale green, nettle-like leaves that are superb for flavouring iced drinks. Put three or five plants in a large tub and pinch out their growing tips. Keep the compost moist: stems and leaves become crisp and dry if their roots are deprived of water. Lift and divide congested plants in spring.

  The form Golden Balm (*Melissa officinalis* 'Aurea') has golden-green leaves and creates a beacon of colour. It is also an excellent herb to use in cooking.
- Rosemary (*Rosmarinus officinalis*): Normally it grows 1.5–1.8m/5–6ft high, but it can be grown in large

CHIVES *are popular in pots. The tubular, mid-green leaves are harvested when young. Rose-pink, starry flowers appear during early and mid-summer, but pinch them off to encourage the development of leaves.*

PLANTERS *with cupped holes in their sides are ideal for collections of herbs, such as Chives, Thyme and Sage. Some planters are formed of plastic, while others are made of reconstituted stone, creating strong containers.*

BAY TREES (Laurus nobilis) *create distinctive features when grown as standards and planted in large pots or tubs painted white. It is a hardy plant, but succeeds best when placed in sheltered corners.*

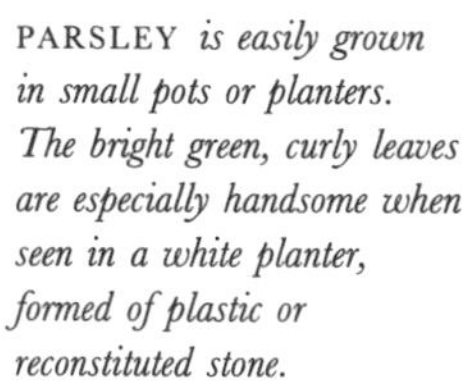

MINT *is an invasive perennial, but a widely-grown and used herb. Try not to mix it with other herbs as it soon suffocates them. Divide plants every two or three years.*

PARSLEY *is easily grown in small pots or planters. The bright green, curly leaves are especially handsome when seen in a white planter, formed of plastic or reconstituted stone.*

THYME *is a perennial and ideal in troughs, pots and planters. It even does well in sink gardens, but remove it if too rampant. Plants often become leggy and unsightly, so divide them regularly.*

tubs and kept shorter by repeatedly pinching out the growing tips of shoots. Plant seven young plants in a tub 45–50cm/18–20in wide.

• Sage (*Salvia officinalis*): This hardy, evergreen shrub eventually forms a domed bush about 60cm/2ft high. However, too often, tall, lanky plants are sold and these never develop into attractive bushes. It is better to buy small plants and when 10–13cm/4–5in high to pinch out their growing tips to encourage bushy growth. When planting into large tubs, use three plants and pinch off flowers to encourage the development of leaves. After three or four years, plants become leggy and are best replaced in spring with fresh ones.

In addition to the ordinary sage, there are several superb forms with coloured or variegated leaves. These include 'Ictarina' (grey-green leaves with yellow variegations) and 'Purpurascens' (better known as the Purple-leaf Sage) with stems and young leaves suffused purple.

OLD PLANT OF THE SEA

Rosemary is said to have gained its name Ros marinus, *which means dew of the sea, from its ability to thrive in areas near to the sea. John Evelyn, the seventeenth-century English garden writer and translator of gardening books, said that its flowers 'are credibly reported to give their scent above thirty leagues [about ninety miles] off, at sea, upon the coast of Spain.' This appears to be a strong claim, but at that time Spanish coastal strips were smothered in the plant.*

Like other herbs, many medical cures were claimed for it, including safe-guarding teeth and encouraging youthfulness.

UNUSUAL CONTAINERS

PERSONALIZING gardens is enjoyable, and on patios this can be done by using unusual containers. The choice is wide, from stacking and securing together a few car tyres, then putting a plastic bucket filled with compost and plants inside it (see page 51), to planting ornate chimney pots. Some ideas are illustrated on these pages, while here are a few others to consider:

- Barrels packed with strawberry plants are a novelty. First, drill drainage holes in the base of a large barrel. Stand the barrel on bricks and then drill 6cm/2½in-wide holes, 15–20cm/6–8in apart, around the sides. Fill the base with 15cm/6in of clean brick rubble. Position a 15–20cm/6–8in-wide tube of wire-netting vertically in the centre and fill it with coarse drainage material. Then, start filling the tub with compost, at the same time planting a strawberry plant in each hole. Fill the barrel to the top, then setting further plants in the compost.
- Old, rectangular, lead water-butts are now rare, but if you inherit one, modify it for plants. Drill or knock holes at its base and sides and fill with 15cm/6in of clean rubble. Top up with compost and plant with some summer-flowering plants, such as pelargoniums and trailing bedding plants.
- Wooden and metal wheelbarrows are novel containers. Drill drainage holes in the base and paint it white. Fill with drainage material, then add compost and summer-flowering bedding plants.
- Plastic, 3.4 litre/six-pint milk containers with the upper part of one side removed – and drainage holes made in the base – can be planted with summer-flowering plants. Eventually, plants smother the container. Suspend them from walls or fences.

IN COASTAL *areas, small, pensioned-off rowing boats create unusual homes for many plants, from small conifers and alpine plants to herbaceous perennials. Drill holes in the boat to ensure good drainage.*

OLD *watering-cans, especially large and galvanized types, are ideal homes for a few upright and trailing plants. Paint the cans white or light green, then stand on bricks or sections of logs.*

AN OLD *wheelbarrow makes an ideal summer home for plants. Ensure it is strong and drill drainage holes in its base. After all risk of frost is over, plant it with a combination of bushy and trailing plants.*

STONE *sinks are ideal for growing alpine plants and small conifers. Traditional ones are best, shallow and hewed out of stone. Deep, glazed sinks can also be used, but need modification* *(see page 50).*

GROWING-BAGS *are recent innovations and have many uses, from growing lettuces and tomatoes to being recycled and used for bulbs and summer-flowering bedding plants (page 55 gives ideas on their reuse).*

SPIRAL *planters create homes for many plants, both around the sides and at the top. On warm patios, small foliage and flowering houseplants can be stood in one. Alternatively, position them indoors.*

- Sections of concrete or fire-brick pipes (about 23cm/9in across and 20cm/8in deep) can be stood on top of each other to form containers 40cm/16in high. Place on a patio or grass, partly fill with coarse drainage material, then add compost. Form small clusters of them and fill with upright and trailing summer-flowering bedding plants.
- Old, strong plastic buckets are ideal for small shrubs and conifers. Remove the handle and pierce holes in the base. They can be camouflaged by painting them, in white or another colour.
- Car tyres can be turned inside out and converted into low containers for spring and summer-flowering plants. Alternatively, cut tyres into three equal parts. Turn each piece so that it forms a container and nail them to a piece of wood that forms a base and holds them upright. To help them harmonize with the rest of the garden, first scrub them and then cover with a matt white paint. Then, pierce holes in their sides, to ensure excess water is able to escape, and fill with compost and colourful plants.

TOILETS AND HELMETS

Although not to everyone's taste, discarded toilets are frequently filled with coarse drainage material, then compost and plants. Choose a range of summer-flowering bedding plants as the main theme, with trailing types around the sides.
Pensioned off war-time metal helmets can easily be converted into hanging baskets. Suspend them from three wires and place trailing houseplants (still in their pots) in the centre. Although they can be filled with compost, this dramatically decreases their life-span. And remember that part of their charm is that their previous use should be easily noticed.

MAKING YOUR OWN CONTAINERS

CONSTRUCTING or modifying containers is not difficult and the three projects suggested here need only a few basic tools, such as a drill, pad-saw and hacksaw, files, pliers, old brush, small trowel, sandpaper and screwdriver, as well as screws and strong wire.

CONVERTING A SMALL BARREL

Small barrels about 60cm/2ft high are easily converted into unusual features on patios. The sequence of tackling this conversion is detailed below. However, a critical factor in step two is to drill the 12mm/1/2in holes near to the edges of the staves, so that after the ends are cut they fall out cleanly.

After completion, paint the barrel. The colours are very much a personal choice, but black for the metal bands and yellow for the wood is one combination.

Cover the drainage holes with broken clay pots, then 5cm/2in of shingle. Fill the rest of the barrel with soil-based potting compost and set summer-flowering plants in it. Alternatively, use more permanent plants such as Houseleeks. Many have very attractive leaves, such as *Sempervivum tectorum* 'Commander Hay'.

CONVERTING A GLAZED SINK

Old glazed sinks can be converted into sink gardens: wash thoroughly, scratch the sides and paint with PVA bonding glue. Mix together equal parts of cement powder, sharp sand and fine peat. Add water to form a paste and cover the sides, top edges and 5cm/2in down into the inside. Allow to dry for several weeks.

Drill three 3mm/1/2in holes and secure with screws.

1. THE *first stage in cutting a 'window' out of a small barrel is to secure the metal bands. In each band, drill two batches of three holes, with 35cm/14in between them. Screw to the wood.*

2. DRILL *four 12mm/1/2in holes in the barrel, 30cm/12in apart but essentially near to the edges of the wooden staves. These holes will form the corners of the 'window'.*

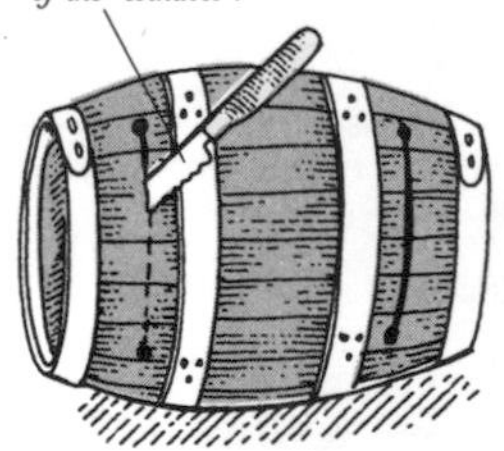

3. USE *a pad-saw to cut out the sides of the 'window'. If the corners are drilled close to the edges of staves, they will then fall out and leave just the two metal bands around the barrel.*

USING OLD CAR TYRES

Unusual containers are easily made from old car tyres. Select three or four equally sized tyres. Secure the bottom tyre to the next one, using three pieces of strong wire (metal coat hangers), then add the next tyre. Place bricks inside the tyres. A large, plastic bucket planted with summer-flowering plants can then be placed inside.

GLAZED SINKS

Shallow, stone sinks are superb as homes for alpine plants, but converted glazed sinks are a good second choice. Thoroughly wash the sink to remove grease and dirt. The method of covering the sink with a rustic, natural-looking, cement coat is detailed on the opposite page. First, however, either place the sink on bricks in its final position, or put two stout poles underneath so that at a later date it can be easily lifted and moved. Completed sinks are very heavy and difficult to lift.

TYRE CONTAINERS

These have great novelty value and are quickly made. Ensure the tyres are all about the same size and not excessively large.

The above illustration details their formation, with a container (large plastic bucket) packed with flowers put in the top. The display can be quickly changed: plant one bucket in late summer with spring-flowering bulbs and biennials, and when this displays fades replace it with another bucket packed with established summer-flowering plants.

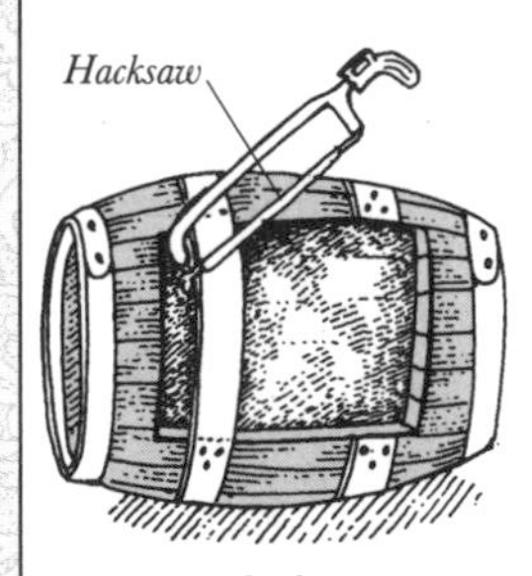

4. USE *a hacksaw to cut the metal bands, close to the staves. When these have been removed, use a file to remove the rough edges of the metal. Then, use sandpaper to smooth them further.*

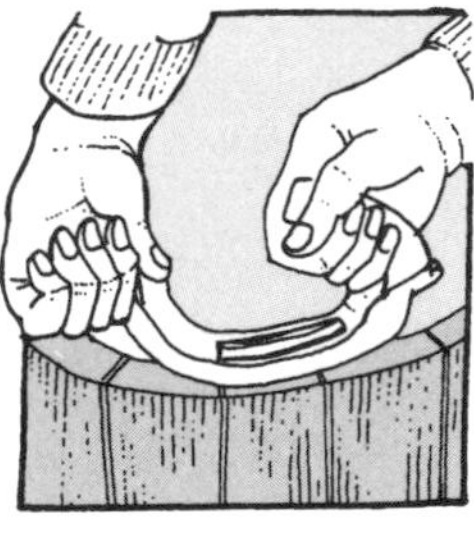

5. THE *two edges that are parallel with the ends also need to be smoothed: first use a coarse wood file or a plane. Afterwards, sandpaper the edges. Drill drainage holes in the base.*

6. EITHER *place the barrel on several bricks, or make a support from short rustic poles secured with cross-halving joints. These are then held together by a strong metal rod.*

MINIATURE WATER GARDENS

WATER gardens in tubs and sinks are unusual and enhance patios beautifully during summer. Unfortunately, because of their relatively small amount of water they are likely to freeze in winter, as well as becoming too hot in summer. Therefore, during warm months they are best positioned in light shade, while in winter they can be taken into cool, frost-proof greenhouses or conservatories. Alternatively, cover the surface with glass. At the same time, insulate the sides with straw and sacking.

SINK PONDS

Water gardens in sinks create fascinating features on patios. Deep stone sinks or modified glazed types (see page 50) are essential to ensure that the depth is sufficient, even for miniature waterlilies. Ensure that the plug hole is waterproofed. Tubs, as well as large metal water casks, can also be used.

LOOKING AFTER THE FISH

Small ponds without fish are rather like birthday cakes without icing. Therefore, put four modest-sized fish in a tub. Because fish are harmed when rapidly transferred between water of differing temperatures, put the fish in a plastic bag (using water from their previous pond) and then place it in the tub. When the water in the bag is at the same temperature as that in the tub, open the bag and gently allow the fish to swim free. However, fish should never be kept in plastic bags for long periods, as they are deprived of oxygen, become overheated, and die.

SELECT *a large tub with strong, metal bands around it. Thoroughly clean the inside and fill with water to swell the wood and make it leakproof. Initially, it may be necessary to keep topping it up with water.*

IF THE *tub continues to leak, line the inside with two layers of polythene. Fill the tub with clean water several times to ensure the liner is clean, then cut off surplus polythene flush to the tub's rim.*

PLANT *waterlilies in plastic-mesh containers. This enables their heights to be adjusted, so that their leaves are not submerged. Also, it is then easier to dismantle and move the display in autumn.*

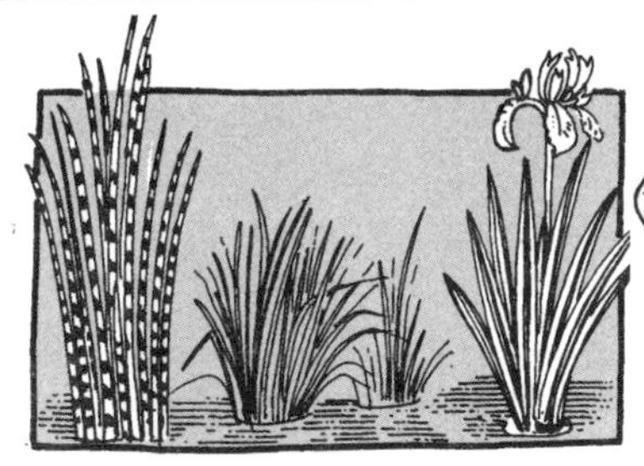

MARGINAL AQUATICS

These are essential, creating the impression of height as well as producing colour and shape constrasts. Select only those plants that are not likely to intrude upon their neighbours. A selection of plants is suggested below.

WATERLILIES

These are delightful in pond containers, but choose only miniature varieties. If too vigorous, the surface is soon covered in leaves and the tub's charm destroyed. There are many to choose from, and several are detailed below.

MARGINAL PLANTS

For a normal-sized pond, there are many water-loving plants to choose from, but in tubs and sinks it is essential to select only those that are non-invasive. Alternatively, keep plants small by dividing them in spring.

- *Carex stricta* 'Bowles Golden': Height 38cm/15in. Beautiful perennial with grass-like, golden-yellow leaves.
- *Iris laevigata* 'Variegata': Height 45–50cm/18–20in. Upright, sword-like, green leaves with silver stripes and soft blue flowers during early summer.
- *Scirpus zebrinus* (Zebra Rush): Height 30–45cm/1–1½ft. Ideal for sink gardens. Perennial, with stems banded in white and green. Divide plants in spring to prevent the development of large clumps.
- *Typha minima* (Dwarf Minima): Height 38–45cm/15–18in. Light green foliage, with flower heads during early and mid-summer.

MINIATURE WATERLILIES

These varieties are suitable for tubs and sinks. The recommended water depth is that between the surface water and the top of the compost in the container, which for small varieties is about 10cm/4in deep.

PONDS: 10–23CM/4–9IN DEEP

- 'Candida' – white and free-flowering variety.
- 'Laydekeri Lilacea' – colour varies slightly, but usually soft to deep rose.
- 'Laydekeri Purpurata' – beautiful, bright wine-red.
- 'Pygmaea Helvola' – small and sulphur-yellow. It is excellent in tubs and skins.

PONDS: 15–30CM/6–12IN DEEP

- 'Caroliniana Nivea' – large, fragrant, white flowers.
- 'Ellisiana' – freely-borne, bright red flowers.
- 'Froebeli' – blood-red.
- 'Indiana' – flowers opening orange-red and maturing to copper-red.
- 'Odorata Minor' – scented and white variety.
- 'Paul Hariot' – flowers open as pale yellow, but with age deepen to copper-red.
- 'Sioux' – flowers open as buff-yellow, but slowly become peach coloured.

PLANTING GROWING-BAGS

GROWING-BAGS offer instant homes to plants. Additionally, they are unique in being both a container and compost. They are used to grow a wide range of plants, including spring-flowering bulbs and summer-flowering bedding plants. Vegetables are also candidates, but only those with fibrous or short roots (see pages 44 and 45).

PLANTING A BAG

Preparing a growing-bag is detailed below. Bags can be placed directly on paving slabs or soil, but placing them on a pallet-like board enables them to be moved and makes it slightly more difficult for slugs and snails to reach the plants.

Piercing four or five holes in a bag's base is often recommended to allow excess water to escape during wet summers, especially when there is only a small amount of leafy growth on plants to use the moisture. If the bag is positioned on soil, holes in the base are possible. Indeed, when growing tomatoes in a bag on soil it is possible to push canes right through the bag's base, providing both drainage and support for the

FLOWERS FOR VASES

Recycled growing-bags are ideal homes for bulbs such as trumpet daffodils that are being grown to produce cut flowers for decoration indoors in spring. Plant large, healthy bulbs (7.5–10cm/3–4in deep and close together) in autumn and place the bag in a sheltered position. Cut the flowers when just starting to open.

GROWING-BAGS, *when stacked in garden centres, inevitably become totally compressed. Therefore, before using one, thoroughly shake the bag to loosen the peat-based compost inside it. Shake it from both ends.*

PLACE *the bag directly on the ground or a flat, pallet-like board. Cut out the windows (along the dotted lines). Some bags have a band that can be slipped over the centre to help restrain the sides.*

SOME *people recommend piercing holes in the bag's base to allow excess water to drain during wet seasons (see above). However, it is always necessary first to moisten the peat-based compost thoroughly.*

FLOWERS IN GROWING-BAGS

Recycling used growing-bags saves money and is environmentally friendly. If used for bulbs, top up with peat in autumn and plant them immediately. For summer-flowering bedding plants, however, store the bag under cover during winter. In late spring, add peat and dust with a general fertilizer. Water the compost and put plants in it as soon as all risk of frost has passed. Use a combination of bushy plants in the centre and trailing ones along the edges to hide the plastic.

plants. However, if the soil is contaminated with pests and diseases, do not pierce the bag, as it could allow their entry. If the bag is on a paved surface, make the slits in its sides and support the plants with a proprietary frame.

When growing spring-flowering bulbs in these bags, make several slits to enable water to escape.

TOPS *of wide walls are ideal places for positioning reused growing-bags. Use low-growing summer-flowering types in the centre and trailers around the edges to cloak the bag's sides.*

FLAT *roofs on garages or home-extensions look bland. In summer, place growing-bags along their edges and pack with plants. In such positions, the compost dries quickly, so water frequently.*

REUSING GROWING-BAGS

As well as putting these bags on walls and flat roofs, they can be used in other ways:

- Recycled bags are especially suitable for growing bulbs, such as daffodils, hyacinths and short-stemmed tulips. Another way is to use them to create a spring hedge of bright-faced yellow daffodils along the side of a patio. Plant the bulbs close together to create a colour-packed display.
- Many herbs are suitable for growing in fresh growing-bags, but those with an invasive nature are ideal for putting in re-used types, where they can be left for several years until either divided or thrown away. Mint, for instance, eventually swamps containers with roots and stems, but in a recycled bag can be left for several seasons. Indeed, the strong roots eventually split the bags.
- At the end of a bag's recycled life, the peat can be either dug into the soil during winter or spread over the surface of borders in spring to create a thick mulch, about 7.5cm/3in deep. First, however, thoroughly water the soil.
- Early potatoes are worth trying in recycled bags: in spring, top up with peat and mix in a general fertilizer. Plant eight tubers of an early variety in each bag.

COMPOSTS, WATERING AND FEEDING

PLANTS in pots, tubs and urns are the athletes of the gardening world: they are expected to perform throughout summer and to create magnificent displays. Many plants do this very well, but they must have the right diet.

COMPOSTS

Plants in containers outdoors are mainly grown in loam-based composts, although those in shallow urns and hanging-baskets are frequently in compost predominantly formed of peat. This is to help retain more moisture in a relatively small root area. Loam, incidentally, is relatively fertile topsoil.

• Shrubs and trees are invariably grown in tubs and therefore a large amount of compost is needed. The loam-based John Innes Potting Compost No. 3 is best and will create a firm base that prevents wind knocking over plants. However, if the cost of buying compost is prohibitive, use equal parts of good garden soil, peat and sharp sand, plus fertilizers.

FEEDING PLANTS

Plants soon exhaust soil of nutrients, especially if the container is small. Once planted, bulbs do not need feeding, nor do biennials. Summer-flowering bedding plants, however, soon use up plant foods and need to be fed every fortnight from mid-summer onwards. Prepare the feed to the manufacturer's recommendation – too strong mixtures may damage or kill plants.

• Herbaceous plants are usually planted in tubs. Although they are not so long-lived as shrubs, each year they develop a vast array of stems and flowers and therefore a good supply of food is essential. Loam-based compost provides food as well as a firm base.

• Bulbs are planted in either loam or peat-based compost. Tall bulbs, such as trumpet daffodils and tulips, need a firm base to support

WHEN *filling a tub, cover the drainage holes with pieces of broken clay pots, then 6–7.5cm/ 2 1/2–3in of shingle or pebbles. Form a thick layer of peat, with loam-based compost on top. This creates a firm base for shrubs and trees.*

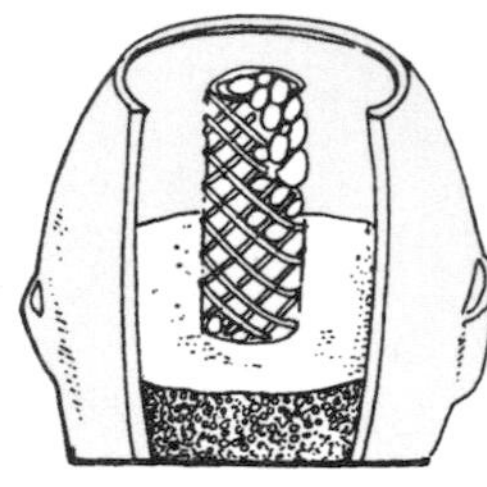

GOOD *drainage is essential in all containers. In barrels and planters, this is achieved by forming a wire-netting tube and filling with coarse drainage material. Place it securely in the container's centre, then add and firm compost around it.*

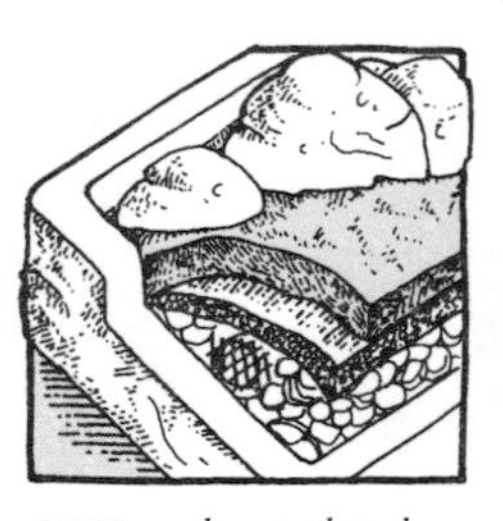

SINK *gardens need good drainage. Place pieces of broken clay pots over the plug hole, then 2.5cm/1in of pea shingle. Over this put 2.5–4cm/ 1–1 1/2in of moist peat, then soil-based compost with extra peat and sharp sand added to it.*

WHEN *groups of pots and tubs are together, it is often difficult to water those at the back without moving them. However, by tying the end of a hose-pipe to a 1.2m/4ft-long cane it is possible to reach them. Never turn the tap on full.*

JUDGING *when plants in pots need water is difficult, but one way to find out if soil in clay pots is dry is to tap the outside with a cotton reel (bobbin) attached to a cane. If the knock creates a ringing note, the compost needs water.*

WHEN *watering plants in pots and tubs, remove the spray from the can and apply water direct from the nozzle. Water the compost gently, so that the surface is not disturbed. Each time water is applied, thoroughly moisten the compost.*

their stems and flowers. And this is best provided by loam-based types. When small bulbs are planted around shrubs in tubs, this invariably is also loam-based. However, low-growing types – when in sheltered places – can be grown in growing-bags which, basically, are packed with peat-based compost.

- Biennials, which are planted in autumn for spring and early summer flowers, are invariably planted in loam-based compost.
- Summer-flowering bedding plants are planted in either soil or peat-based compost. If the container has little space for compost, the peat-based type is better, as it retains more moisture.
- Rock garden plants in sink gardens need a well-drained mixture formed of loam-based compost, peat and sharp sand.

WATERING PLANTS

Knowing when to water plants and how much to give them is, perhaps, one of the most difficult gardening skills to master. If too much is given, plants wilt and eventually die; if excessively watered, compost becomes saturated, with the subsequent risk of roots being killed and plants wilting. The best general watering guide for plants in containers outdoors is to wait until the surface compost starts to dry, then thoroughly soak it. Soil-based compost, when dry, is easier to re-soak than peat types, which appear to resist water.

WATERING PLANTS

Watering plants in gardens and pots has always been an art, but perhaps never more so than during the mid-fifteenth century with this perforated clay pot. Once full, it continuously spouted water until exhausted.

WINTER PROTECTION

WHEN shrubs and trees are grown in border soil in gardens, excess water can usually drain away. Even when these plants are growing in tubs and pots there is not a problem during summer, when they are growing strongly and using the moisture in their growth processes. During winter, however, when plants are not active, excess water remains in the compost. This may cause roots to rot, as well as increasing the chance of the compost freezing during excessively cold periods.

In earlier years, during winter the compost was covered by pieces of slate or tiles, but nowadays it is easier to use thick polythene. Covering a tub is detailed below: cover the compost for as short a time as possible. Wait until the worst of the winter rains have arrived, and remove as soon as the weather improves. If left in place for too long in spring, the compost may remain too dry to encourage early growth. Fruit trees grown in large pots and tubs are especially vulnerable to the compost remaining dry at a time when moisture is essential to encourage the development of flowers and fruit buds. If the compost does become dry, thoroughly water it.

WATER-SHEDDING ROLE

Apart from being fundamental in the growth processes of plants, leaves also direct rain that falls on them to the area where the fibrous, food and moisture-absorbing roots are situated. This is normally just at the extreme edges of the canopy created by the leaves. Therefore, where evergreen shrubs and trees are in tubs – and their canopy extends beyond the tub's edges – the risk of compost becoming too wet in winter is not great. Small evergreen shrubs and deciduous types are most at risk from excessive rain in winter.

COMPOST *in tubs can become too wet in winter unless covered. Place bricks or pieces of wood on either side of the stem or trunk and spread a sheet of thick polythene over them and the compost. Cut the polythene so that it fits around the stem.*

DRAW *the polythene up around the stem and tie it in a collar. Take care not to damage the stems or trunk by securing it too tightly. The polythene must be slightly higher than the rim, to ensure that water runs off and not back towards the centre.*

FORM *the polythene into neat pleats around the tub's sides. Tightly tie the polythene around the sides, then use sharp scissors to trim it about 7.5cm/3in below the string. Remove the polythene in late winter or spring.*

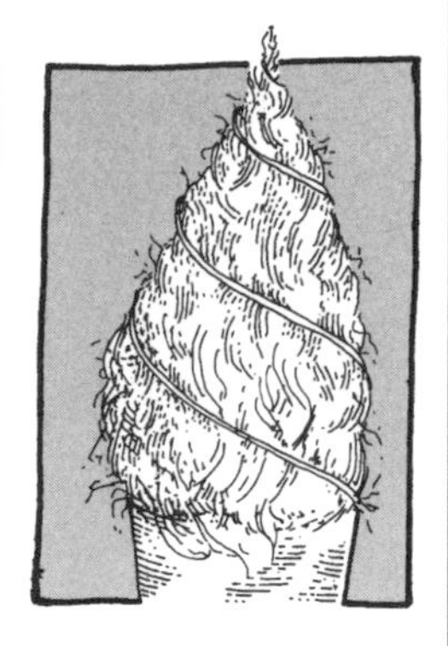

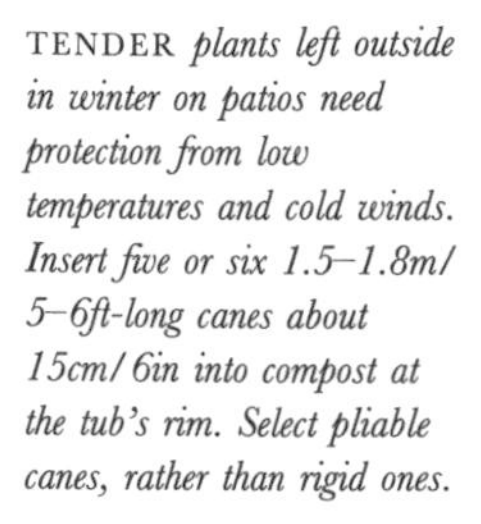

TENDER *plants left outside in winter on patios need protection from low temperatures and cold winds. Insert five or six 1.5–1.8m/ 5–6ft-long canes about 15cm/6in into compost at the tub's rim. Select pliable canes, rather than rigid ones.*

DRAW *the canes together at the top and tie them securely. If necessary, bow them out slightly so that they completely encircle the foliage. Ensure they are secure, as they must create a framework that when covered resists strong gusts of wind.*

TIE *a long piece of string to the top and pack straw or hay around the upper parts of the canes. As straw is put in position, twist string around in a descending spiral. Add more straw, securing it with string, until the plant's base is reached.*

SURVIVING COLD WINDS

Young, tender, evergreen shrubs growing in tubs are susceptible during winter to damage from cold winds. Apart from moving these plants to sheltered positions, they can be temporarily clad in straw or hay. The method of doing this is detailed above.

Wait until the onset of really cold weather before covering the shrub, and remove the cover as soon as the risk of cold winds decreases. It is essential during this period that air should not be totally excluded from the shrub. Plants that are tightly covered create havens for overwintering insects, as well as encouraging the onset of diseases in early spring.

In addition to a straw covering, cold winds can be deflected by erecting a canvas screen on the windward side. Alternatively, sandwich straw between two layers of stiff wire-netting. This can be bent to assume a curved shape and put around the plants.

EARLY PROTECTION

Before the introduction of polythene, the compost in large tubs was kept dry and warm by using two large tiles or slates. These had to be at least the width of the tub or pot, and about two-thirds of the width in depth. On one long side of each tile a half-circle was removed, so that it fitted snugly around the stem. The tiles were then leaned against the stem to deflect rain-water off the compost.

CONTAINER GARDENING CALENDAR

SPRING

This is the season of preparation, with many plants raised in gentle warmth in greenhouses in early spring, ready for planting into containers in late spring or early summer. Never put tender plants outside before the risk of frost has passed. Similarly, do not plant herbaceous plants into containers too early.

- Sow summer-flowering bedding plants in gentle warmth in early spring (16 to 23).
- From early to late spring, slowly accustom summer-flowering bedding plants to outdoor temperatures (16 to 23).
- In late spring, plant summer-flowering bedding plants into containers. In cold areas, it is best to leave this job until early summer (16 to 23).
- In late spring, sow biennials, such as Polyanthus and Wall-flowers, outdoors in seed-beds to produce plants for planting into containers in late summer or early autumn (14).
- Sow seeds of half-hardy climbers in spring. Later, slowly acclimatize them to outdoor conditions and plant into containers as soon as all risk of frost has passed (36–37).
- Plant sink gardens in spring in cold areas (40–41).
- Sow carrots in containers at any time from mid-spring to mid-summer (44–45).
- Sow French beans in containers on patios in late spring (44–45).
- Put young climbing bean plants in containers on patios during late spring (44–45).
- Sow radishes in containers on patios during mid and late spring (44–45).

SUMMER

Many areas are not free from frost until early summer, and this therefore delays planting and establishing half-hardy summer-flowering plants. However, once planted they soon become established and, if regularly watered and fed, create a display throughout summer, until the onset of frosts in autumn. Regularly check the compost in tubs where herbaceous perennials are growing to ensure it is moist. Also, feed them regularly.

Remove dead flowers from all plants to encourage the development of further ones.

- In late summer, plant spring-flowering bedding plants into containers (14–15).
- In early summer, sow biennials such as Daisies and Forget-me-nots outdoors in seed-beds for planting into containers in late summer or early autumn (15).
- Plant geraniums (Pelargoniums) into containers as soon as all risk of frost has passed (24–25).
- Plant tender fuchsias into containers outdoors as soon as all risk of frost has passed (24–25).
- Feed fuchsias throughout summer (24–25).
- Sow carrots shallowly and thinly in containers from mid-spring to mid-summer (44–45).
- Put young climbing bean plants in containers on patios during early summer (44–45).
- Sow radishes shallowly and thinly in containers on patios during early summer (44–45).
- When watering groups of pots, tie a cane to the end of a hose-pipe (56–57).
- Feed summer-flowering plants throughout summer (56–57).

AUTUMN

Wash and place unused containers under cover during winter. Types formed of thin plastic are especially vulnerable to wet and frosty winter weather.

Autumn is the time to renovate wooden containers. The bases of tubs eventually rot away: transfer the plants to other containers and clean out the tub. If the sides are strong and intact, the base can usually be repaired. Paint all new wood with a plant-friendly wood preservative.

Plant herbaceous perennials into containers in autumn in areas with warm winters. Alternatively, wait until spring.

After all summer-flowering plants have been removed and their pots stored away, wash down the patio with a moss-remover, then thoroughly rinse.

- In early autumn, plant spring-flowering bedding plants into containers (14–15).
- Move geraniums (Pelargoniums) into greenhouses or conservatories (24–25).
- Place growing-bags under cover, in a dry place, as soon as summer flowers and vegetable crops have been removed. These bags can be reused during the following year (54).
- Plant daffodils in several layers in tubs to create a feast of colour in spring (42–43).
- In autumn, tidy up hardy herbaceous perennials by cutting off dead stems. Cover the compost of slightly tender plants with straw to prevent their roots being damaged by low temperatures.
- Plant sink gardens in autumn in mild areas (40–41).
- Plant daffodils in growing-bags in late summer or early autumn to produce cut flowers for home decoration (54).

WINTER

This is the time for planning arrangements of plants for the forthcoming season, as well as ordering the seeds of half-hardy, summer-flowering bedding plants. Mixing and matching these plants is detailed on pages 16 to 23, together with many examples of exciting combinations.

Snow is a danger to shrubs and trees in containers; if the covering is too thick it weighs down stems, causing permanent damage if left on them too long. Use a stick or round piece of plastic piping to gently knock off the snow.

When birds and squirrels have exhausted their natural food in gardens and hedgerows, during cold winters they then devour practically anything – even on patios. For that reason, it is better to feed them regularly.

If tall plants are blown over, stand them up immediately. If left on their sides, they eventually become misshapen and never recover their former outline. In exposed areas, always put tall plants in heavy tubs.

In exceptionally exposed areas, put pots with tall plants in clusters to afford them slight protection from the strong winds.

- Move miniature water gardens planted in sinks or tubs into greenhouses during winter. Alternatively, cover with glass, straw and sacking (52–53).
- In excessively wet and cold areas, cover the compost in large tubs with polythene (58–59). But remove it during late winter or early spring.
- Protect tender evergreen shrubs in tubs and other containers by forming a wigwam of canes and straw around them (58–59). Remove this protective covering as soon as the risk of cold winds has passed.

USEFUL CONTAINER GARDENING TERMS

ALPINE PLANTS: *Plants native to zones officially classified as between the upper limits of trees and the permanent snow line. These plants are frequently used to create miniature gardens in shallow stone sinks.*

ANNUAL: *A plant that is raised from seed and completes its life-cycle within one year. Some annuals are half-hardy and raised in gentle warmth in spring. These are planted into containers in late spring and early summer.*

BARRELS: *Initially, these were used to transport beer or wine. When old they are sold and converted into tubs or containers for strawberries.*

BIENNIAL: *A plant that takes two seasons to grow from seed and to produce flowers. Many spring-flowering bedding plants grown in containers are biennial, such as Daisies.*

BULB: *Formed of overlapping, fleshy, modified leaves, creating a food-storage organ that, when given the right conditions, develops leaves and flowers. Many spring-flowering plants in containers are bulbs, such as Hyacinths and Daffodils.*

BULB PLANTERS: *These are cask-like, with cupped holes around the sides into which bulbs can be planted. There is also space at the top. Larger plants are used for strawberry planters and herbs. They are formed of several materials, including plastic and reconstituted stone.*

COADE STONE: *Terracotta-type, artificial stone made during the late 1700s and early 1800s. Containers made of this material are prized.*

COURTYARDS: *Originally, open areas surrounded by buildings or walls, perhaps inside a castle. Nowadays, they are usually paved areas at the rear of a building and surrounded by a wall.*

CROCKS: *Broken pieces of clay pots used to cover drainage holes in containers.*

DEAD-HEADING: *The removal of faded flowers to encourage the development of further ones.*

DECIDUOUS: *Trees and shrubs that shed their leaves in autumn and develop fresh ones in the following spring.*

EVERGREEN: *Trees and shrubs that appear to retain their leaves throughout the year, although some are continually being shed.*

EXOTIC PLANTS: *Correctly means plants from other parts of the world, but more frequently applied to colourful and unusual plants.*

FIBREGLASS: *A modern, durable material, with fibres held together by a resin. It is used to form a wide range of containers for plants.*

GLAZED SINKS: *These were fitted into many kitchens during the earlier part of the 1900s. They have a glazed surface and can be modified to accommodate plants.*

GROWING-BAG: *Originally introduced to grow tomatoes, but now widely used for flowering plants and vegetable crops.*

HALF BARREL: *See Tub.*

HARDENING OFF: *Acclimatizing plants to outdoor conditions in spring and early summer. Plants, such as half-hardy annuals, are raised in gentle warmth in late winter or early spring, and slowly become accustomed to outdoor conditions.*

HERBACEOUS PERENNIALS: *Plants that die down to soil level in autumn and send up fresh shoots in spring. Many low-growing types can be grown in large tubs.*

HERBS: *Plants with culinary or medicinal values. Many of the low-growing types are suitable for growing in pots and tubs.*

JARDINIERE: *A large, decorative stand or pot, used to display plants.*

JOHN INNES COMPOSTS: *Loam-based composts originated during the late 1930s at the John Innes Horticultural Institution, Britain. They standardized composts for sowing seeds, as well as potting and repotting plants.*

LOAM-BASED COMPOSTS: *Composts formed mainly of fertile top-soil, with the addition of sharp sand, peat and fertilizers. They form heavy bases for large plants in containers.*

PATIOS: *The Spaniards use this term to describe an inner court open to the sky and surrounded by a dwelling. They introduced the term to North America, where it came to mean any paved surface around a home. The term later migrated to Britain and became widely used.*

PEAT-BASED COMPOSTS: *Composts formed mainly of peat, with the addition of fertilizers.*

PEDESTALS: *Used to support urns as well as ornaments. They vary in height, from 60cm/2ft to about 1.5m/5ft.*

PLASTIC: *Versatile, modern material used to make many containers for garden plants.*

PRICKING OFF/ PRICKING OUT: *Transferring seedlings from where they were sown into seed-trays or pots and given far more space in which to grow larger.*

RECONSTITUTED STONE *Used to form a wide range of plant containers, as well as ornaments. It mellows to a pleasing colour.*

REUSED GROWING-BAGS: *Growing-bags used during one season can be topped up with peat and fertilizers during the following one and used to grow summer-flowering bedding plants and bulbs.*

SHRUB: *A woody plant with several stems arising from ground level.*

SINK GARDENS: *A way to grow small plants, such as miniature conifers and alpine plants, in stone sinks.*

SINK PONDS: *Miniature water gardens formed in a deep stone, or a modified glazed sink. Miniature ponds can also be made in wooden tubs.*

SPRING-FLOWERING BEDDING PLANTS: *These are usually biennials, sown in late spring or early summer in seed-beds outdoors and planted into containers in autumn for flowering during the following spring.*

STANDARD: *Plants with long stems between the ground (or pot's surface) and the lowest branches or shoots. This distance varies widely, according to the type of plant.*

STANDARD FUCHSIAS: *A way of growing fuchsias, with stems from 15cm/6in to 107cm/42in long.*

STONE SINKS: *Old sinks, usually shallow, frequently used to create miniature gardens for alpine plants, small bulbs and miniature conifers.*

STRAWBERRY BARRELS: *A traditional way of growing strawberry plants: holes are cut in a large barrel and strawberry plants planted into compost placed inside it.*

SUMMER-FLOWERING BEDDING PLANTS: *Plants raised from seeds sown in gentle warmth in early spring and planted into containers when all risk of frost has passed. In autumn, they are discarded.*

TENDER PERENNIALS: *Perennial plants – such as pelargoniums and most fuchsias – that are not sufficiently hardy to be left outside all through the year.*

TERRACES: *Open, paved areas immediately outside a house. Sometimes, they are on several levels, united by a flight of steps.*

TERRACOTTA *(also* TERRA-COTTA*): A hard, brownish-red material formed of clay, fine sand and occasionally pulverized pottery waste. This is made into containers – usually unglazed – for plants.*

TOP-DRESSING: *Shrubs and trees in tubs cannot be repotted (and thereby given fresh nutrients) so the surface compost is removed in spring and replaced with fresh. Do not damage the roots.*

TREE: *A woody plant with a single, clear stem between the roots and lowest branches.*

URN: *A vase of varying shape and ornamentation – made of stone, metal, plastic or fibreglass – in which plants are grown. Because of their usual shallow size and therefore the limitation on the amount of compost that they can contain, they are mainly used for summer-flowering plants.*

VERANDAH (VERANDA): *Term derived from India, where it is found in several native languages and describes a gallery at ground level on one side of a house or, sometimes, surrounding it. The roof slopes to shed water and is open partly or wholly on the garden side.*

VERSAILLES PLANTER: *A large, square-sided container originated at Versailles. Early ones were made of lead or slate, while modern ones are wood or fibreglass.*

INDEX